TOP **10**
SINGAPORE

JENNIFER EVELAND
&
SUSY ATKINSON

EYEWITNESS TRAVEL

Left **Siloso Beach** Center **Orangutans at Singapore Zoo** Right **Esplanade – Theatres on the Bay**

LONDON, NEW YORK,
MELBOURNE, MUNICH AND DELHI
www.dk.com

Design, Editorial, and Picture Research by
Quadrum Solutions, Krishnamai, 33B, Sir
Pochkanwala Road, Worli, Mumbai, India

Reproduced by Colourscan, Singapore
Printed and bound in China by
Leo Paper Products Ltd

First American Edition, 2009
09 10 9 8 7 6 5 4 3 2 1

Published in the United States by
DK Publishing, Inc., 375 Hudson Street,
New York, New York 10014

ISSN 1479-344X

ISBN 978 0 7566 4566 3

Within each Top 10 list in this book, no hierarchy
of quality or popularity is implied. All 10 are, in
the editor's opinion, of roughly equal merit.

Floors are referred to throughout in accordance
with British usage; ie the "first floor" is the floor
above ground level.

> **We're trying to be cleaner and greener:**
>
> • we recycle waste and switch things off
> • we use paper from responsibly managed
>   forests whenever possible
> • we ask our printers to actively reduce
>   water and energy consumption
> • we check out our suppliers' working
>   conditions – they never use child labour
>
> **Find out more about our values and
> best practices at www.dk.com**

Contents

Singapore's Top 10

The information in this DK Eyewitness Top 10 Travel Guide is checked regularly.
Every effort has been made to ensure that this book is as up-to-date as possible at the time of
going to press. Some details, however, such as telephone numbers, opening hours, prices,
gallery hanging arrangements, and travel information are liable to change. The publishers
cannot accept responsibility for any consequences arising from the use of this book, nor for
any material on third party websites, and cannot guarantee that any website address in this
book will be a suitable source of travel information. We value the views and suggestions of
our readers very highly. Please write to: Publisher, DK Eyewitness Travel Guides,
Dorling Kindersley, 80 Strand, London WC2R 0RL.

Left **Lanterns inside Thian Hock Keng Temple** Center **Chinese Garden** Right **Elgin Bridge**

Left **Underwater World** Right **Statue of Sir Thomas Stamford Raffles at his landing site**

 Key to abbreviations
Adm *admission charge* **Dis. access** *disabled access*

3

SINGAPORE'S TOP 10

SINGAPORE'S TOP 10

🔟 Singapore's Highlights

At the crossroads of East and West, Singapore has a complex mix of culture and history. At first glance, the city appears to be wholly modern with soaring skyscrapers, but a closer look reveals the legacies of its Eastern and European heritage. The grand Neoclassical buildings of the Colonial District stand alongside the ethnically diverse neighborhoods of Chinatown, Little India, and Kampong Glam, with the Singapore River carving its way between them. It is a multi-faceted city with both traditional and contemporary appeal.

National Museum of Singapore

The ideal introduction to Singapore and its multitude of cultural influences, the newly refurbished National Museum *(left)* presents history using interesting multimedia displays *(see pp8–9).*

Singapore River

Once the lifeline of the island's early settlers, the Singapore River is lined by countless waterside dining and leisure establishments, most in old converted warehouses. It is best experienced from aboard a restored bumboat *(right)* *(see pp10–11).*

Thian Hock Keng Temple

This is Singapore's first Chinese Taoist temple and is undoubtedly one of its finest *(above).* It is a good starting point for exploring the many wonders of Chinatown. Since 1839, it has been an important cultural icon for the city's Chinese inhabitants *(see pp12–13).*

Sultan Mosque

With its gold onion domes *(left)* that rise above Kampong Glam, the city's traditional Muslim quarter, Sultan Mosque is a fine blend of Persian, Moorish, and Turkish design. It is the heart of the local Muslim community *(see pp14–15).*

Little India

SERANGOON ROAD
SUNGEI RD
ROCHOR CANAL RD

FORT CANNING RD

PRINSEP ST
BENCOOLEN STREET
MIDDLE ROAD
SELEGIE RD
VICTORIA ST
BRAS BASAH ROAD
NORTH BR

STAMFORD ROAD

HILL STREET
RIVER VALLEY ROAD

Colonial Quarter

ST ANDREW'S RD
Padang

Empress Place

HAVELOCK RD
EU TONG SEN STREET
NEW BRIDGE ROAD
NORTH CANAL ROAD
UPPER PICKERING ST
SOUTH BRIDGE RD
CHURCH STREET
COLEYER QUAY

Chinatown

CROSS STREET

Marina Bay

TANJONG PAGAR RD
MAXWELL ROAD
RATTLES QUAY

500 ⊢ yards ⊣ 0 ⊢ meters ⊣ 500

Sri Veeramakaliamman Temple

5 Statues of Hindu gods crowd this temple's roof *(above)*, where they watch over Little India. Dedicated to the deities Vinayagar, Viswanathan, and Kali, this 1881-built temple is one of Singapore's oldest *(see pp16–17)*.

Singapore Botanic Gardens

6 On sprawling grounds just beyond the city center, the beautifully maintained botanic gardens *(right)* are especially refreshing in the early mornings when the air is cooler *(see pp18–19)*.

Singapore Zoo and Night Safari

7 A perennial tourist favorite, this award-winning zoo is recommended for adults as well as children. The Night Safari *(left)* is the world's first for viewing nocturnal animals in settings much like their natural habitat *(see pp20–21)*.

Singapore Flyer

8 The largest observation wheel in the world *(right)* looms high above Marina Bay. It offers incredible views over the Singapore River, from the nearby Colonial District out to neighboring islands visible in the distance *(see pp22–3)*.

Raffles Hotel

9 This grand hotel *(below)* represents the unending romance of colonial exploration that helped to build early Singapore, and the drive for absolute luxury that characterizes its success. The hotel has its own museum *(see pp24–5)*.

Sentosa

10 Singapore's popular playground, Sentosa *(above)* is an island of relaxing spas and resorts, thrilling water and land sports, and other attractions for people of all ages *(see pp26–7)*.

🔟 National Museum of Singapore

The colonial splendor of the National Museum, unveiled on Queen Victoria's Golden Jubilee in 1887, reflects the British empire at its most confident. Following Singapore's independence in 1965, the building was developed as a monument to the country's history and culture. Behind the original building is a modern wing. Its glass and steel structure is a striking contrast to the original restored building. The galleries make creative use of design, lighting, and interactive exhibits to tell Singapore's story.

Video installations in the Living Galleries

🎦 Admission to the Singapore Living Galleries is free 6–8pm daily.

🍴 The museum has several cafés, bars, and restaurants offering snacks or formal Chinese and European dining.

- Map L1
- 93 Stamford Rd.
- 6332-3659
- Open 10am–6pm daily (Singapore Living Galleries stay open until 8pm)
- Adm S$10 adults, S$5 children (free admission for children 6 years and below), students, and senior citizens
- Disabled access
- www.national museum.sg

Top 10 Features

1. Architecture and Design
2. The Glass Passage
3. Multimedia Displays
4. Singapore History Gallery
5. Gallery Theatre
6. Singapore Living Galleries
7. Fashion Gallery
8. Film & Wayang Gallery
9. Food Gallery
10. Photography Gallery

1 Architecture and Design
Built to Sir Henry McCallum's design in 1887, the Neo-Palladian architecture *(above)* was joined in 2006 by a stunning Modernist structure that more than doubled the size of the original building.

2 The Glass Passage
The construction of the glass passage is an architectural achievement and a visually stunning link between old and new. It provides a close view of the old dome and its Victorian stained-glass panels.

3 Multimedia Displays
Interactive displays play a vital role here. The Singapore History Gallery *(left)* is enriched with sound effects, while the Food Gallery smells of the fruit and spices of Singaporean cuisine.

 Sir Frank Swettenham's portrait by John Singer Sergeant, in the Singapore History Gallery, is valued at more than S$4 million.

4 Singapore History Gallery
A spiral path leads to the last fragment of the 14th-century Singapore Stone *(below and see p11)*. Ceramics, jewelry, and coins indicate trading before Stamford Raffles reached the island.

5 Gallery Theatre
The museum holds regular film screenings, theater performances, and retrospectives in its 250-seat theater.

6 Singapore Living Galleries
Four interesting permanent galleries in the old wing comprise the Fashion Gallery, Film & Wayang Gallery, Food Gallery, and Photography Gallery. Visitors can view the restored stained glass of the dome *(see below)* before entering the galleries.

7 Fashion Gallery
This gallery looks at the nation's love affair with shopping. Its displays also, quite importantly, highlight the role of dress as an expression of changing national identity in Singapore.

8 Film & Wayang Gallery
Three screens here show interesting excerpts of early Singaporean cinema. One of the rooms has displays of Wayang (Chinese opera) costumes and hair ornaments, and a puppet theater.

9 Food Gallery
This gallery explains how Singaporeans have easily adapted traditional dishes of immigrant cultures. Favorites like *roti prata* (Indian flat bread with gravy) and *nasi lemak* (Malaysian coconut rice) are the results of culinary intermingling.

Key

▬	Basement
▬	Ground Floor
▬	First Floor
▬	Second Floor

10 Photography Gallery
A century of history is revealed in wedding portraits and family snaps *(left)*, alongside personal filmed accounts of Singapore life. This gallery has on display one of the earliest known photographic images of Singapore, taken in 1844.

Restoration and Expansion

The museum's dome is the clearest sign of a painstaking restoration, begun in 2004 and completed in 2005. Victorian stained-glass panels were restored and invisibly reinforced. In the new wing, it took a year just to design the Glass Passage, but the results have been hailed as a superb marriage of contrasting architectural styles. A team of curators is seeking new exhibits and treasures to display here.

The Singapore River

Flowing past the 1920s godowns (warehouses), the bars and restaurants of Clarke Quay, and the skyscrapers of the financial district, the Singapore River has always been at the center of city life. The river, which forms a natural harbor, was the first to attract Sir Thomas Stamford Raffles, the city's founder. A walk along the banks is the best way to enjoy some of Singapore's iconic views. Better still, step aboard one of the bumboats that once jostled for space around Boat Quay. Since an intensive clean-up operation in 1987, the river has become the city's emotional heart. It may no longer be the main artery of commerce, but it has moved on from its frenetic and polluted heyday.

Elgin Bridge

🚤 Bumboats may look touristy but they are the best way to appreciate the city's skyline.

🍽 The outdoor terrace at Indochine, next door to the Asian Civilisations Museum, offers a stunning view of Boat Quay and the Central Business District. Arrive early to get a good table.

• Bumboat tours depart from Parliament House Landing Steps, by Raffles Landing Site: Map L3
• Asian Civilisations Museum: Map M3, 1 Empress Place; 6336-9050; open 1–7pm Mon, 9am–7pm Tue–Sun, 9am–9pm Fri; Adm; www.acm.org.sg
• Old Parliament House: Map M3, 1 Old Parliament Lane; 6332-6900; open 10am–9pm daily; events ticketed; www.theartshouse.com

Top 10 Features

1. Raffles' Landing Site
2. The Merlion
3. Cavenagh Bridge
4. Asian Civilisations Museum
5. Old Parliament House
6. Boat Quay
7. Elgin Bridge
8. Clarke Quay
9. G-MAX Reverse Bungy, GX-5 Xtreme Swing
10. Robertson Quay

Raffles' Landing Site
The spot at which Sir Thomas Stamford Raffles landed is commemorated by a marble statue *(below)*, a cast of the bronze original at the Victoria Theatre and Concert Hall. It is framed to the north by the Colonial District and to the south by the Central Business District towers.

The Merlion
Half-fish and half-lion, the Merlion symbolizes the unity of the lion city and the sea. Guarding the river like an ancient mythical beast, the Merlion was created by the Singapore Tourist Board in 1964. The current statue was unveiled in 1972.

Cavenagh Bridge
Designed as a draw-bridge and built in Glasgow, this bridge was named after a former governor of Singapore. Long since pedestrianized, a Victorian sign forbids the passage of cattle and horses.

Look out for the bronze statues of jumping children and Singaporean "drain cats" at Cavenagh Bridge.

Asian Civilisations Museum
Built in 1867, these former government offices were renamed the Empress Place Building in the early 1900's, and reopened as the Asian Civilisations Museum in 2003 (see p36).

Old Parliament House
Singapore's oldest building (left), erected in 1827, was named Parliament House after Singapore gained its independence in 1965 (see p34).

Boat Quay
The quay (below) hasn't stopped buzzing since Chinese merchants first built godowns here in 1820. Most of the boats have gone and the quay is lined with bars and restaurants.

Elgin Bridge
The oldest crossing point of the river was but a wooden drawbridge in 1822. The current bridge, completed in 1929, is named after the Earl of Elgin, Governor General of India in the 1960s.

Clarke Quay
Singapore's favorite evening spot, Clarke Quay is the river's largest conservation project. Godowns (below) have been stylishly renovated to create a fashionable hub of waterfront bars and restaurants.

G-MAX Reverse Bungy, GX-5 Xtreme Swing
Thrill-seekers can fling themselves skywards for an alternative view of the Colonial District. Bungy jumping is only recommended for those with a strong heart.

The Singapore Stone
On display in the National Museum (see p9), this piece of inscribed sandstone remains a mystery. Part of a rock discovered at the mouth of the river in 1819, its 50 lines of inscription eluded translation by scholars including Raffles. The rock was blown up in 1843 on the orders of a British engineer. This fragment is the only surviving relic.

Robertson Quay
As trade grew, swampland upriver was reclaimed and used to build godowns, creating Robertson Quay. The area is now a metropolitan waterfront scene, with chic restaurants, bars, and galleries.

10 Thian Hock Keng Temple

Built in 1839, this is one of Singapore's oldest Chinese temples. It was raised by sailors in homage to the goddess Ma Zu, who, it is believed, laid down her life to give seafarers a safe passage. The temple, paid for by individual donors such as Hokkien leader Tan Tock Seng, was constructed in the southern Chinese architectural style. It is laid out along a traditional north-south axis, with shrines to several deities. The temple underwent a facelift in 2000.

The Chung Wen Pagoda

Ma Zu, the Guardian of the South Seas

🌸 Thian Hock Keng celebrates festivals such as the Chinese Lunar New Year and the birthdays of Guan Yin and Ma Zu with prayer, traditional music, and dance. Since all Chinese holidays are guided by the lunar calendar, it is best to ask the temple exactly when these holidays fall.

🍴 At the corner of Telok Ayer and Amoy streets, a popular hawker center offers cold drinks, local dishes, and fruit.

- Map L4
- 158 Telok Ayer St.
- 6423-4616
- Open 7:30am–5:30pm daily
- www.thianhockkeng.com.sg

Top 10 Features

1. The Front Step
2. Construction
3. Door Paintings
4. The Ceiling
5. Ancestral Tablets
6. Ma Zu, the Guardian of the South Seas
7. Guan Yin, the Goddess of Mercy
8. Statue of Confucius
9. Statue of Chen Zhi Guang
10. Chong Hock Girls' School

The Front Step
The temple was originally located by the river, but land reclamation has cut it off from the sea. This raised step protected it from the tide that once lapped at its foundations.

Door Paintings
Paintings on the door depict auspicious creatures *(above)*. In Taoist tradition, these protect the temple. A plank across the threshold keeps ghosts away, and ensures visitors bow heads upon entering.

Construction
Craftsmen from Southern China built the temple *(above)* in the traditional manner using no nails. All the materials required for building it were imported from China, including ironwood for the pillars and pottery used in the roof's mosaics.

The Ceiling
During the renovation of the temple in 2000, artists from China were brought in to restore the carvings on the ceiling under the main altar, replacing the gold leaf and bright paint.

5 Ancestral Tablets

In keeping with the Taoist practice of ancestor worship, ancestral tablets *(above)* inscribed with the names and dates of departed devotees, are regularly tended with offerings of incense, food, and prayers.

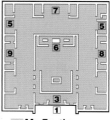

6 Ma Zu, the Guardian of the South Seas

The main hall contains an image of Ma Zu, the sea goddess. She was born in AD 960 in China's southern Fujian province, and risked her life to save fishermen and sailors.

7 Guan Yin, the Goddess of Mercy

In the courtyard behind the main altar sits Guan Yin *(above)*, the Goddess of Mercy. She is said to have rejected nirvana to return to earth especially to help the needy and unfortunate.

8 Statue of Confucius

Confucius *(below)*, one of China's greatest thinkers (551-497 BC), developed a social value system that promoted education, self-discipline, respect for family, and political responsibility – values that continue to shape Chinese society today.

9 Statue of Chen Zhi Guang

This 8th-century Chinese governor was so successful in developing the economy and improving living standards that the Hokkien people came to worship him as a deity.

10 Chong Hock Girls' School

The temple housed one of Singapore's first girls' schools, funded by the Huay Kuan, a Hokkien community association. Such clan associations were the backbone of the local Chinese.

Etiquette in Chinese Temples

As in any place of worship, respect for devotees deep in prayer is appreciated. Photography is permitted but visitors must refrain from touching anything on altars. Unlike Hindu temples or Muslim mosques, clothing norms here are relaxed. Shorts and sleeveless tops are allowed and footwear can be worn inside the temple.

For more Singapore places of worship See pp38–9

🔟 Sultan Mosque

The Sultan Mosque is at the heart of Singapore's Muslim community. It is located in the neighborhood that, in 1819, was assigned to the Malay Sultan of Johor and the temenggong (chief) of Singapore. The original mosque that stood on this site was constructed in 1824. Partially funded by the East India Company, it resembled the style of mosque typically found in Southeast Asia, with a low two-tiered roof like a pyramid. A century later, the old mosque had fallen into a state of disrepair and planning for a replacement began. Design for this structure was entrusted to Denis Swan, an Irish architect with Swan & McLaren, the local architecture firm responsible for many landmark buildings.

The royal graves at the maqam behind the mosque

🐦 After sunset during Ramadan, the month of fasting, the streets fill with stalls and stores selling delicious Malay treats.

🍵 Sip Turkish or Malay-style tea or fresh lime juice in one of the cafés along the shady, palm-fringed Bussorah Mall, located opposite the mosque.

- Map H5
- 3 Muscat St.
- 6293-4405
- Open 9am–12:30pm, 2–4pm Mon–Thu, 2:30–4pm Fri–Sun

Top 10 Features

1. Architectural Design
2. The Bottle Band
3. The Domes
4. Mosque Alignment
5. Ablutions
6. The Central Prayer Hall
7. The Mimbar
8. The Mihrab
9. The Maqam
10. The Annex

1 Architectural Design

The mosque is built in Saracenic style, combining Persian, Moorish, and Turkish design including pointed arches, minarets, and domes. The interior is adorned with calligraphic verses and mosaics.

2 The Bottle Band

Around the base of the main onion dome is an unusual architectural feature. It is a wide black band made from rows of bottles stacked on their sides, five or six bottles high. Their bottoms appear to glisten like black and brown jewels in the sun.

3 The Domes

A tradition in mosque architecture, the onion dome originates from Turkey and the Middle East. It creates a roofline distinguishable above the city's low-rise buildings. At the top of the gold domes *(left)* is the star and crescent – a traditional symbol of Islam.

4 Mosque Alignment

Most mosques are built with the prayer hall facing the holy Muslim city of Mecca. For this reason, North Bridge Road has a distinct bend to allow for the correct alignment of Sultan Mosque.

5 Ablutions

Two areas have faucets, for worshipers to wash before prayers. Ablutions, or *wudhu* *(above)*, is a ritual to purify the body and soul.

6 The Central Prayer Hall

Large enough to accommodate 5,000 devotees, the main hall *(center)* is for men only, while female worshippers occupy the galleries above. The carpet, donated by a Saudi Arabian prince, bears his emblem.

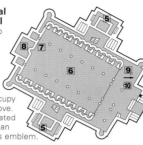

7 The Mimbar

On Fridays, the Muslim holy day, the imam is known to deliver his sermon, or *khutba*, to a prayer hall packed full of devotees. He does so from the *mimbar*, an elaborate pulpit atop a staircase reserved for the purpose *(below)*.

8 The Mihrab

The *mihrab* is a small niche that marks the direction of Mecca, and from where the imam leads the congregation in prayer five times a day. It is surrounded by motifs and represents a doorway to the holy city.

9 The Maqam

At the rear of the mosque is a *maqam*, or mausoleum, with graves of important local community members, including the grandson of Sultan Hussein, who signed over Singapore to Raffles in 1819.

10 The Annex

Mosques serve many purposes for Muslims – providing space for schools, religious celebrations, and fundraising. The annex at the Sultan Mosque *(left)*, built in 1993, offers similar services to the local Muslim community.

Mosque Etiquette

Non-muslims are welcome to visit the mosque, but are not permitted to enter the main prayer hall. Viewing is allowed from the surrounding courtyard and corridors. Appropriate dress, such as pants or long skirts and shirts with sleeves, is required for men and women. The mosque provides robes at the entrance for visitors dressed inappropriately. Footwear must be removed outside.

For more Singapore places of worship See pp38–9

🔟 Sri Veeramakaliamman Temple

In the mid-19th century, Indian laborers, who settled in what is now Little India, built a Hindu shrine there. The original temple, a small nondescript structure, was demolished in 1983 to make way for the one that stands here today. It took three years to build at great cost, with artisans brought from India. The Sri Veeramakaliamman Temple is dedicated to the goddess Kali, which is why Hindus who worship here leave with red ash smeared on their foreheads; those who pray at temples for male deities receive white ash. This is one of Singapore's oldest temples and remains popular with local Indians.

Idol of Kali

🕯 During Deepavali *(see pp44-5)*, the most significant holiday for local Hindus, the temple is illuminated with tiny candles, symbols of the eternal light of the soul.

☕ Across the street at the Norris Road Coffee Shop you can watch fresh *chapatis* (Indian bread) being made and order cheap curries to go with them.

• Map F3
• 141 Serangoon Rd.
• 6295-4538
• Open 5:30am–noon, 4–9pm daily
• www.sriveerama kaliamman.com

Top 10 Features

1. Kali
2. The Gopuram
3. Smashing Coconuts
4. Muruga
5. Roof Figures
6. The Altar of the Nine Planets
7. Ganesh
8. Sri Periachi
9. Washing of the Deities
10. Sri Lakshmi Durgai

1 Kali
Kali, occupying central position on the main altar, is the Divine Mother. She represents the cycle of birth through death – her name comes from the Sanskrit for "endless time." She is also known as the Destroyer of Evil.

2 The Gopuram
Row upon row of figures, representations of deities, top the *gopuram* or main gate *(center)* and the roof. On holy days, when the temple is full, devotees can appreciate these images from outside.

3 Smashing Coconuts
Before entering the temple, devotees smash coconuts *(left)* in a small metal box. This is symbolic of shattering their obstacles to spiritual concentration. These coconuts even have "eyes" carved into them, which are meant to "see" the obstacles in a devotee's path and destroy them.

Muruga
Muruga is the name given to the God of War – the six-headed deity who grants great success to his devotees. He is mostly worshipped by Tamils, who form the majority of the city's Indian population.

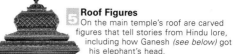

Roof Figures
On the main temple's roof are carved figures that tell stories from Hindu lore, including how Ganesh *(see below)* got his elephant's head.

The Altar of the Nine Planets
Each planet is represented on this altar *(left)*, at which devotees pray to their zodiac sign. Jewelry stores nearby sell rings adorned with nine stones, placed according to the astrological alignment of each wearer.

Ganesh
Distinguishable by his elephant's head, Ganesh *(below)* is the most worshipped of all Hindu deities. As the Remover of Obstacles, he is invoked at the start of prayers to help clear the mind, and consulted at the beginning of any new ventures by devotees.

Sri Periachi
In one corner of the compound a dais holds the statue of the fierce Sri Periachi *(above)*. Despite being depicted amid blood and gore, she is the goddess of fertility, safe childbirth, and the good health of newborn babies.

Washing of the Deities
On the right side of the main altar, a small spout serves the purpose of draining the water that has rinsed the deities during their morning cleansing ritual *(below)*. This water is considered holy and used in prayer.

Sri Lakshmi Durgai
While many Hindu figures and deities appear aggressive, Sri Lakshmi Durgai is represented as beautiful and graceful. According to Hindu belief, the goddess's three eyes and 18 arms will bring peace and joy to those who pray to her.

Etiquette in Hindu Temples

Visitors must remove footwear before they enter, and wear appropriate attire – legs must be covered, and shirts should at least have short sleeves. In Indian culture, the left hand is reserved for toilet tasks, so pointing toward a person or sacred object with the left hand is impolite. If you must point, use your open hand. You should also turn off cell phones before entering.

For more Singapore places of worship **See pp38–9**

Singapore Botanic Gardens

This extensive park is one of the finest botanical gardens in Southeast Asia. Pathways meander through a tropical landscape that showcases the region's natural habitats and species. There are avenues of frangipanis and scarlet lipstick palms, and wide, sloping lawns adorned with trees and sculptures. On weekends, the gardens are a magnet for families, joggers, and dog walkers. During the week, it is an oasis of calm in the city. The park was founded in 1859 as a pleasure garden. It has also played a role in the production of cash crops, including spices and rubber.

Fun adventures in the children's playground

🎵 The Singapore Symphony Orchestra plays free outdoor concerts at the amphitheater. Check www.sbg.org.sg or contact the information desk for events.

🍴 Halia, surrounded by the greenery of the Ginger Garden, is a great spot for lunch.

- Map S2
- Cluny Rd.
- 6471-7361
- Open 5am–midnight daily
- Adm free except Orchid Garden: adults S$5, senior citizens S$1, children free
- www.sbg.org.sg

Top 10 Features

1. National Orchid Garden
2. Vanda Miss Joaquim
3. The Marsh Garden
4. The Spice and Herb Garden
5. Sculptures
6. Rain Forest
7. The Lakes
8. The Sundial Garden
9. The Ginger Garden
10. Children's Playground

1 National Orchid Garden

This beautiful enclosure with over 1,000 orchid species and 200 hybrids is the fruit of 80 years' work. The hybrids are named in honor of VIPs, royal visitors, and political alliances. It is the only area with an admission fee (see p42).

2 Vanda Miss Joaquim

There is debate over whether this hybrid of pink, violet, and orange-rose was discovered or bred by Miss Agnes Joaquim in 1893. It is a lovely orchid *(left)*, and was chosen as Singapore's national flower in 1981.

3 The Marsh Garden

This area displays water-loving plants at their best. A natural depression has been turned into a pond with lilies *(right)*, papyrus, Siamese screw pines, and the indigenous scarlet-leafed Sealing Wax Palm.

4 The Spice and Herb Garden

A fascinating, fragrant area, this garden showcases the spices that formed the backbone of Singapore's early trade, including cloves, pepper, cinnamon, lemongrass, nutmeg, and several species of ginger.

5 Sculptures

Several sculptures by Sydney Harpley near the bandstand celebrate the families who come to play on weekends. Favorites include *Joy (left)*, *The Girl on a Bicycle* who freewheels along the top of a spiral hedge, and *Girl on a Swing* who pauses mid-air.

6 Rain Forest

The park's first designers recognized the importance of the indigenous forest and preserved an area of rain forest, where ancient trees *(above)* continue to thrive today.

7 The Lakes

The gardens have three lakes. Swan Lake is named for its Australian swans while ducks and herons enjoy Eco Lake. Concerts by the Singapore Symphony Orchestra *(see p85)* are staged at Symphony Lake *(above)*.

8 The Sundial Garden

This formal garden *(center)* is named for its sundial, which is surrounded by four symmetrical pools. You will often see brides and grooms being photographed here.

9 The Ginger Garden

More than 250 species of ginger are displayed here, along with other ornamental and edible species, including lilies and turmeric. The waterfall *(below)* provides a great photo opportunity.

10 Children's Playground

At the Jacob Ballas Garden, children under 12 are encouraged to discover life sciences through play, and to investigate the role of plants and water in everyday life. Carry sunscreen and a change of clothing.

"Mad" Ridley

Henry Ridley, a young British botanist, became the first director of the Botanic Gardens in 1888 and spent the next 23 years developing their horticultural potential. In the late 19th century, he devised a way to tap rubber without damaging the trees. Convinced by the crop's potential, he lobbied planters so zealously that he became known as "Mad Ridley." A sculpture dedicated to his work can be seen in the gardens.

Singapore Zoo and Night Safari

One of the island's most visited sights, the Singapore Zoo and Night Safari offer the chance to see more than 3,200 animals living in spacious enclosures designed to resemble their natural habitats. They are often grouped with other species with which they would have coexisted in the wild. The zoo is sensitive to conservation and environmental concerns and now focuses on animals best suited to Singapore's climate. Interactive exhibits, shows, programs, and informative signs, all in English, educate visitors about the animals and their behavior.

A colorful macaw

Observing Malayan tapirs at the Night Safari

🐾 A store within the zoo handily sells insect repellent and sunscreen.

🍽 Dine on Asian and Western food, indoors or alfresco. The "Jungle Breakfast" is served 9–10am daily.

- Map S1
- 80 Mandai Lake Rd.
- 6269-3411
- Zoo: open 8:30am–6pm daily; adm S$18 adults, S$9 children; tram S$5 adults, S$2.50 children; shows all day; www.zoo.com.sg
- Night Safari: open 7:30pm–midnight daily; hourly shows 7:30–9:30/10:30pm Fri–Sat; safari stores & restaurants open 6pm; park gates open 7:30pm; adm S$22 adults, S$11 children; tram S$10 adults, S$5 children; www.nightsafari.com.sg
- Park Hopper ticket: allows a visit to both parks, once each, over a month; S$30 adults, S$15 children

Top 10 Features

1. The Open Zoo
2. Jungle Breakfast
3. Elephants of Asia
4. Orangutan Exhibit
5. Amphitheaters
6. Night Safari
7. Asian Zone
8. Trails
9. South American Zone
10. African Zone

1 The Open Zoo
Enclosures at the open zoo *(above)* avoid the use of cages. Animals here are separated from visitors, and each other, by dry and wet moats. The more dangerous animals live in landscaped areas, viewed through glass walls.

2 Jungle Breakfast
Visitors are invited to join playful orangutans and other friendly residents for breakfast, one of the zoo's most popular activities. This is also the best time to visit the zoo, while the air is still cool.

3 Elephants of Asia
This display is designed to resemble the type of logging camp found in Myanmar (Burma). Visitors can ride on Asian elephants *(left)* or observe them from elevated boardwalks.

Of the Top Ten features, entries 1–5 are in the zoo; entries 6–10 are in the Night Safari.

Orangutan Exhibit 4

The zoo is home to 24 Southeast Asian orangutans *(right)*, living as a community within a large enclosure with climbing platforms, trees, vines, and thick foliage.

Night Safari 6

With over 1,000 animals, this night zoo and wildlife park allows visitors to observe animals at night, when they are most active. It also stages shows, such as the Thumbuakar performance *(center)*.

Amphitheaters 5

The Shaw Foundation Amphitheatre stages a rain forest show and The Splash Amphitheatre features a "Splash Safari" with marine animals. Both focus on wildlife conservation.

Asian Zone 7

Of the Night Safari's eight geographic zones, six are Asian. They protect animals that have been hunted almost to extinction, such as the Malayan tiger *(below)*.

Trails 8

Three footpaths – the Fishing Cat Trail, the Leopard Trail, and the Forest Giants Trail – offer a closer look at nocturnal animals. You can view leopards, flying squirrels, and mouse deer.

South American Zone 9

Species such as the capybara *(right)*, the world's largest living rodent, and the giant anteater, live within an area that replicates the dense rain forests of South America.

African Zone 10

In the Equatorial Africa zone, landscaped to resemble the African savannah, visitors will see cape giraffes *(left)*, the world's tallest animals; servals, which are night-time predators; and bongos (forest gazelles).

Park Guide

The Singapore Zoo and Night Safari are two separate parks located side by side. Both are operated by Wildlife Reserves Singapore. While the zoo is best toured on foot, there is also a tram at extra cost. Visitors can also take a tram at the Night Safari, although this is not included in the entry fee either. It operates an enjoyable circular route, with a number of stops at which visitors can alight and explore the trails.

 The Rainforest Kidzworld playground has outdoor activities, plus a fountain lagoon with slides for all ages. Bring swimming gear.

🔟 The Singapore Flyer

The city's newest attraction and the world's tallest observation wheel, the Singapore Flyer (center) offers 360-degree views of the city and environs, including neighboring Indonesia and Malaysia. The wheel's 28 air-conditioned capsules can hold up to 28 passengers each, and reach a height of 541 ft (165 m). On a clear day, you can see for nearly 30 miles (48 km). According to Buddhists, the round shape of the wheel is auspicious for Singapore and its motion is positive feng shui. The following sights can all be viewed from the top of the wheel.

Passengers inside one of the capsules

🌐 The shopping mall at the foot of the Flyer has a number of restaurants and cafés, plus gift shops and a spa.

🍴 Gelatissimo serves refeshing gelato alfresco at the foot of the Flyer.

- Map P3
- 30 Raffles Avenue, #01-07
- 6333-3311
- Shuttle bus from Coleman Street beside St. Andrew's Cathedral every half hour from 10am to 11pm; bus no. 111, 106, or 133 from Bras Basah Rd.
- Open 8am–10pm daily
- Adm: Adult S$29.50; senior S$23.60; child S$20.65
- www.singaporeflyer.com

Top 10 Features

1. Marina Bay
2. The Skyline
3. The Singapore River
4. The Padang
5. Keppel Harbour
6. Shipping Lanes
7. East Coast Neighborhoods
8. Kallang River Basin
9. Kampong Glam
10. Indonesia and Malaysia

1 Marina Bay

A massive barrage project, to be completed in 2009, will dam Marina Bay and create a freshwater reservoir in the city. A development of office towers, luxury residential high-rises, and 24-hour leisure facilities will surround the bay.

2 The Skyline

Singapore's tallest skyscrapers *(below)*, the OUB Centre, UOB Plaza One, and Republic Plaza, rise above Shenton Way, the city's downtown financial district, while the water's edge is flanked by low-rise heritage buildings.

3 The Singapore River

The river *(see pp10–11)* bisects the city's down-town, separating the Shenton Way business district from the buildings around the Padang. Old godowns now serve as a riverside leisure center.

The Padang

While the Padang, or playing field, cannot be seen itself, visitors can view the heritage buildings around it, such as the Old Parliament House, the former Supreme Court, St. Andrew's Cathedral, and the Esplanade – Theatres on the Bay *(above)*.

Keppel Harbour

For over a century this port has operated shipping facilities and served as a link between downtown businesses and industries on the island's West Coast.

Shipping Lanes

The endless stream of tankers and small ships plying the waters around the island *(above)* are a sight to behold as they head to and from the world's busiest port.

East Coast Neighborhoods

Government housing and condominium towers *(above)* blanket the city. But among these are culturally significant heritage neighborhoods, such as Katong and Geylang.

Kallang River Basin

To the east of the Flyer is the Kallang River, which is great for watersports such as sea kayaking and waterskiing. Beside the river, the Singapore Indoor Stadium has restaurants and cafés along a wide promenade.

Indonesia and Malaysia

To the south of Singapore, islands belonging to Indonesia can be seen beyond the shipping lanes. To the east are the conical mountains that belong to the Malaysian state of Johor.

Kampong Glam

The golden domes of Sultan Mosque *(below)* gleam in the sunlight in the neighborhood of Kampong Glam – Singapore's Islamic quarter and the traditional heart of its Muslim life.

Singapore's Big Plans

At the time of writing, much of what is seen from the Flyer is construction activity. In 2009, the Marina Bay Sands resort will open beside Marina Bay, introducing casinos to Singapore. The US$3.6-billion facility will have dining and shopping areas, and convention space. The first phase of the Financial Centre is scheduled to open in 2010.

🔟 Raffles Hotel

Behind the famous façade of Singapore's grandest old lady is a labyrinth of tropical courtyards and verandas. Raffles Hotel was founded by the Armenian Sarkies brothers in a beachfront bungalow in 1887. It was saved from the city's perpetual modernization when it was declared a National Monument during its centennial. Following a multimillion-dollar renovation, the hotel is once again the epitome of colonial grandeur. With a range of restaurants, boutiques, galleries, bars, and its own museum, Raffles is much more than the sum of its elegant parts; it is a destination in its own right.

Jubilee Hall

🕐 If a Sling's not your thing, try a Million Dollar cocktail or sample a Shanghai Lily, inspired by the painting displayed behind the Long Bar.

🍴 For an early breakfast in late-rising Singapore, Ah Teng's Bakery serves good coffee and great pastries from 7:30am.

- Map M1
- 1 Beach Rd.
- 6337-1886
- Museum: open 10am–7pm daily
- www.singapore. raffles.com

Top 10 Features

1. The Hotel
2. The Long Bar
3. Architectural Restoration
4. Bar & Billiard Room
5. Writer's Bar
6. Restaurants and Bars
7. Gift Shop
8. Jubilee Hall
9. Raffles Culinary Academy
10. Museum

① The Hotel

Character and opulence come at a price, but few hotels can match Raffles' blend of history, luxury, and colonial ambience. The hotel's famous and exotically dressed Sikh doormen are charming and patient with photo requests.

② The Long Bar

Birthplace of the Singapore Sling, this bar *(left)* must be the only spot in the city where guests are encouraged to litter peanut shells. Singapore Slings are often pre-mixed, but if the bar is quiet, ask for a fresh cocktail.

③ Architectural Restoration

It took three years and S$160 million to restore Raffles Hotel to its position as the Queen of Singapore's luxury hotels. Inspired by its 1900s heyday, the revamped hotel and Raffles Arcade were unveiled in 1991, with new stores and extra suites.

Bar & Billiard Room

Legend has it that Singapore's last tiger was shot under the billiard table in 1902. Billiards *(above)* has given way to buffets, but you can still bag a Tiger in the form of a popular beer.

Writer's Bar

A quieter place to sip a Sling, this elegant bar is located in the hotel's colonial lobby. Browse the works of former guests Somerset Maugham, Joseph Conrad, and Rudyard Kipling. The resident pianist plays a range of musical genres.

Restaurants and Bars

All Raffles' restaurants maintain high standards in food-obsessed Singapore. Refuel with pastries at Ah Teng's Bakery, or enjoy the signature dishes at the Raffles Grill *(above)*.

Gift Shop

The Raffles palm motif adorns everything, from slippers to hats, in the hotel's extensive gift shop *(above)*. Fancy bottles of pre-mixed spirits for creating Singapore Slings make a compact memento.

Jubilee Hall

Designed by theater specialist Charles Cosler of New York, this Victorian-style playhouse theater within Raffles Arcade is a popular venue for plays, recitals, and films. A list of events is available at the hotel's front desk.

Museum

Raffles' small museum focuses on the hotel's early days until its restoration and opening, and gives a fascinating picture of pre-war Singapore. Photographs, letters, and travel memorabilia celebrate the hotel's glory days.

Raffles Culinary Academy

Rudyard Kipling urged Victorian travelers to "feed at Raffles," but today's patrons can take a more active role. Courses at the on-site academy *(below)* range from wine appreciation to master classes by world-renowned chefs.

Top 10 Famous Guests

Raffles' celebrity guest list includes writers, actors, and singers from every era. The literary tradition began with Joseph Conrad and Rudyard Kipling, who were early guests, followed by Somerset Maugham. In the 1950s, Anthony Burgess stayed en route to Malaya. Old Hollywood stars, such as Charlie Chaplin and Maurice Chevalier, were followed by Noel Coward, Ava Gardner, and Elizabeth Taylor in the post-war years.

🔟 Sentosa

Sentosa is Singapore's pleasure island – a local getaway dedicated to recreation. Although mocked as "Disneyesque," it is a well-planned resort with varied attractions that should appeal to everyone. The beaches may be man-made, but they are clean and pleasant, with plenty of bars, restaurants, and facilities nearby. The island was originally called Pulau Blakang Mati, meaning "death from behind," possibly because of the pirates that once attacked its shores. It was later renamed Sentosa, which means "peace and tranquillity."

The Merlion

Travelator at the Underwater World

🏖 Tanjong Beach has the best sunset views on the island.

🍴 Coastes, overlooking Siloso Beach, is a versatile choice, serving drinks and international food from morning till night.

- Map S3, T3
- Sentosa Island
- 1800-736-8672
- Adm S$3 (3 years and above). If driving, S$2 per car and S$2 per person in the car
- Open 24 hours daily
- www.sentosa.com.sg

Top 10 Features

1. Images of Singapore
2. Underwater World
3. Sentosa Luge & Skyride
4. Sentosa 4D Magix
5. Nature Walk
6. Siloso Beach
7. Fort Siloso
8. Sentosa Golf Club
9. Spa Botanica
10. Cable Cars

1 Images of Singapore

This museum *(below)* pays homage to Singapore's history and diversity. Kids will love the cleverly designed special effects, which give a sense of the values shaping Singapore society *(see p37)*.

2 Underwater World

Visit early to enjoy the walk-through shark tank and marine displays here. The spa offers "fish reflexology," where fish nibble at your toes before their human counterpart takes over for a therapeutic pummelling *(see p50)*.

3 Sentosa Luge & Skyride

A cross between a toboggan and a go-cart, the luge *(right)* is great fun for all ages. Take the Skyride chairlift to the top of the hill and meander your way back down again. Each cart has sophisticated speed controls for safety.

Sentosa 4D Magix
Billed as Southeast Asia's first 4D theater, Magix features a state-of-the-art digital projection system, surround-sound, and seats that move with the on-screen action. The effects include mist spray in water scenes.

Nature Walk
If lucky, you may spot long-tailed macaque monkeys, wild white cockatoos, and insect-eating pitcher plants on this walk through Sentosa's forest. Though not comparable with reserves like Bukit Timah (see p97), the half-hour walk is worth the effort.

Siloso Beach
This beach (center) is where the young and beautiful hang out, sunbathing and playing volleyball. Several beach bars and stores operate during the day, although the pace – and volume – picks up at sunset.

Fort Siloso
Original features at this fort are enhanced to re-create the life of colonial soldiers (above). Special effects include battle sounds and re-creations of Japan's surrender (see p40).

Sentosa Golf Club
Home to two attractive and challenging courses with great views over the harbor, the Tanjong course features natural lakes and an undulating fairway. The Serapong course is home to the Singapore Open.

Spa Botanica
This spa in Sentosa's lush gardens has been repeatedly voted one of the best in the world. Signature therapies include jasmine body scrubs and papaya wraps, followed by aloe vera facial treatments.

Cable Cars
The most exciting way to arrive at Sentosa is by cable car. Standard or glass cabins swing from Mount Faber or HarbourFront over the water to Imbiah Lookout. The views of the world's busiest port and nearby islands are stunning.

Travel Tips

The Sentosa Express monorail is fast and cheap. It runs from VivoCity shopping mall to two stations. Free red, yellow, and blue buses ply around Sentosa from 7am to 11pm (Sun–Thu) and 7am to 12:30am (Fri–Sat). Private cars, buses, and taxis can cross to Sentosa using the causeway. Car and taxi passengers must pay the entrance fee at booths near VivoCity.

Left **Re-creation of surrender to Japan in 1942** Right **The inauguration of the Suez Canal in 1869**

🔟 Moments in History

1 1390: Iskandar Shah
A deposed prince called Iskandar Shah declared himself ruler of the island of Temasek. Legend has it he saw a lion-like creature and renamed the island *Singapura*, or lion island. The Keramat at Fort Canning is said to be his tomb (see p42).

2 1819: Arrival of Sir Stamford Raffles
On a mission to find the East India Company new trading sites, Stamford Raffles stepped ashore at Singapore. Convinced it could be a strategic trade site, he persuaded its leaders to sign a treaty giving exclusive rights to Britain.

Portrait of Sir Thomas Stamford Raffles

3 1824: British East India Company
The East India Company secured undisputed legal rule of the island. Tariff-free trade was enticing and the village quickly became a town. In 1826, Singapore was declared capital

Parliament's first meeting in 1965

of the Straits Settlements and became a flourishing Crown Colony by 1867.

4 1869: Suez Canal
The opening of the Suez Canal in Egypt in 1869 transformed Singapore's trading potential by opening new markets and reducing travel distance between Europe and Asia.

5 1873: Steam Ship Travel
The development of steam ships brought more reliable shipping schedules. Singapore quickly became a major refuelling port, employing thousands of porters to heave coal.

6 1907: Rubber and Tin
New technologies demanded new materials. Rubber seedlings grown in the Botanic Gardens were used to create Singapore's first rubber plantation. Meanwhile, the first smelter for producing tin opened at Pulau Brani to satisfy the demands of America's new canning industry.

7 1942: World War II
After a Japanese attack sank HMS *Repulse* and the *Prince of Wales*, British forces retreated down the Malay peninsula, blowing up the causeway to delay the invasion. Singapore fell on February 15, 1942, and an

Former Prime Minister Lee Kuan Yew

estimated 50,000 people, mainly Chinese Singaporeans, died during Japan's three-year occupation of the island.

1959: Singapore's Self-Government

After years of negotiation, the British agreed to hold general elections, resulting in a victory for the center-left People's Action Party, which promised a Singapore united with Malaya and fully independent of Britain.

1959: Lee Kuan Yew

Lee Kuan Yew became the island's first prime minister on June 3, 1959. Revered by many as the father of the nation, Lee stepped down in 1990 but remains a towering figure in Asian politics. He now acts as Minister Mentor to the current leader, his son, Lee Hsien Loong.

1965: Singapore's Independence

Singapore became part of the Federation of Malaysia in 1963. However, political and racial tensions led to riots in 1964 and on August 9, 1965, Lee announced a separation and the Republic of Singapore was born.

Top 10 Singapore Reads

1 King Rat by James Clavell
Drawing on his experience as a Changi POW, Clavell's novel weighs the costs of survival.

2 Lord Jim by Joseph Conrad
When the crew of a stricken ship abandons its passengers, one officer is left to answer for his actions.

3 Saint Jack by Paul Theroux
A tale of an ageing, seedy expatriate on the make.

4 The Singapore Grip by JG Farrell
A satirical novel about a privileged expatriate family on the eve of the Japanese invasion.

5 Snake Wine: A Singapore Episode by Patrick Anderson
Anderson presents a picture of a 1950s Singapore that is now almost unrecognizable.

6 First Loves by Philip Jeyaretnam
Tales of life in Singapore's cultural melting pot.

7 Little Ironies: Stories of Singapore by Catherine Lim
Short stories that look at Singaporean life and society.

8 The Singapore Story: Memoirs of Lee Kuan Yew
Singapore's first PM lists the events that shaped a nation.

9 A History of Singapore by C. M. Turnbull
Tracing Singapore's history from Raffles' arrival to 1988.

10 Rogue Trader by Nick Leeson
An account of how Leeson lost a billion, and spent four years in Changi prison.

Left **Lion dance during Chinese New Year** Right **Traditional Malay headscarves on sale**

Ethnic Groups

The Chinese – Hokkiens
The majority (78 percent) of Singaporeans are ethnic Chinese. Of these, 41 percent are the Hokkien dialect group from China's southern Fujian province. They were the earliest Chinese immigrants and built the Thian Hock Keng Temple *(see pp12–13)*.

The Chinese – Teochews and Other Dialect Groups
Other Chinese groups include the Teochews and Cantonese, from China's Guangdong province, who make up 21 and 15 percent of the Chinese community. Their contributions to local culture include cuisine and opera.

The Malays
Although Malays are Singapore's native inhabitants, today they are a minority

Hindu priest and worshiper at a temple

A Peranakan woman

comprising 14 percent of the population. The term "Malay" should not be confused with "Malaysian": Malay is a race; Malaysian is the nationality of Singapore's northern neighbors.

The Peranakans
Also known as "Straits Chinese," a Peranakan is a person born in colonial Southeast Asia to a Chinese father and non-Chinese mother. Fluency in many languages and cultures made them locally prominent. Their culture is celebrated at the Peranakan Museum *(see pp36–7)*.

The Indians – Hindus
Indians first came to Singapore as early as Raffles *(see p30)*. Many were businessmen or financiers who contributed to Singapore's progress. Today, Indians (more than half of whom are Hindus) make up 9 percent of the population.

The Indians – Sikhs
Originating from the Indian state of Punjab, the Sikhs are a small yet visible group, identifiable by their turbans. Their reputation for bravery inspired the British to employ Sikhs for security work.

The South Asians – Muslims
Muslims comprise a quarter of the Indian population. Most are Tamils from southern India and

Friday prayers at the Sultan Mosque

northern Sri Lanka. Tamil is one of the official languages of Singapore, in addition to English, Malay, and Mandarin.

The Eurasians
In colonial times, marriages between Europeans and locals created mixed-heritage families who developed their own unique traditions. Today, though many locals are considered Eurasian by race, their heritage is dying out with the older generation.

The Arabs
Singapore's Arab community is small but influential. Most Arabs came from Hadramaut in Yemen, heading trading firms and undertaking philanthropic projects, such as building schools and welfare associations.

The Expatriates
Almost 20 percent of the population is made up of non-resident workers, mostly people from the Philippines, Indonesia, and Bangladesh who work in industries shunned by locals. White-collar workers come from North America, Australia, and Europe, but the most significant number is from China and India.

Top 10 Words in "Singlish" – the local Patois

1 aiyoh
The Chinese Mandarin exclamation of surprise or concern.

2 Alamak
The Malay exclamation of surprise or concern, meaning "Mother of God."

3 Ang moh
From the Chinese Hokkien dialect, *ang moh* ("red hair") is the local slang for Caucasian. It is not usually derogatory.

4 chope
Chope means "to reserve." A common way to *chope* a table in a food court is to place a tissue packet on it.

5 die-die
From the English word "die," this means to be absolutely certain.

6 face
Stands for reputation or status, as in "save face" or "give face" – Chinese concepts developed to show respect for superiors.

7 goondu
Literally "heavy stone" in Tamil, *goondu* means "idiot."

8 kiasi
Meaning "fear of death," *kiasi* describes one who is afraid to take risks.

9 kiasu
From the Chinese Hokkien word for "fear of losing," *kiasu* describes one who is afraid of losing out to someone else. *Kiasi* and *kiasu* are often-cited characteristics of the typical Singaporean.

10 lah
Lah along with *lor*, *meh*, and *mah*, are words used in sentences for emphasis.

33

Left **CHIJMES** Right **City Hall with the Supreme Court beyond**

🔟 Architectural Sights

1 Old Parliament House

Singapore's oldest building, dating from 1827, was mistakenly built as a private residence on a spot reserved for government use and subsequently taken over by the colonial administration. Designed by G. D. Coleman, a popular architect, the Neo-Palladian style incorporated verandas, high ceilings, and porticos. However, renovations over the years have almost obliterated the original design *(see pp10–11)*.

2 Empress Place Building

In 1867, the government built the Empress Place to house its administrative offices. Placed at the mouth of the Singapore River, the Neo-Palladian structure was one of the first things newcomers to the city would see on arrival. In the 1980s, it was converted into the Asian Civilisations Museum, its design surviving four major extensions over the years *(see pp10–11)*.

3 Victoria Theatre and Concert Hall

This ornate structure was designed in the Italian Renaissance style popular in Victorian England at the time. The Theatre, originally a Town Hall, was finished in 1862. In 1905, the Memorial Hall was added to honor Queen Victoria. Today, this national monument is the venue for the Singapore Symphony Orchestra *(see p85)*.

4 City Hall and Supreme Court

The wide stairs and columns of this building are in a style that was standard for government structures when it was built in the 1930s. Beside it, the former Supreme Court has a dome like St. Paul's Cathedral in London. Both will become the National Art Gallery in 2012. ⊗ *Map M2* • *3 St. Andrew's Rd.* • *No public access*

5 St. Andrew's Cathedral

Resembling an English parish church, this Anglican church, consecrated in 1862, is made of *chunam*, a paste of shell lime, egg whites, and coarse sugar mixed with boiled coconut husks. The recipe was imported from British India and applied by Indian convict laborers. ⊗ *Map M2* • *11 St. Andrew's Rd.* • *6337-6104* • *Open 9am–5pm Mon–Fri, 9am–1pm Sat* • *www.livingstreams.org.sg*

Row houses at Emerald Hill Road

Shophouses are row houses with a shop at the front, which were introduced to Singapore by Chinese immigrants.

The Esplanade – Theatres on the Bay

6 CHIJMES (Convent of the Holy Infant Jesus)

This convent was originally built in 1841, and an orphanage was added in 1856. In 1903 a chapel was added, lending a Gothic touch with arches and columns. In 1983, the convent made way for clubs and restaurants.

Ⓢ *Map M1* • *30 Victoria St.* • *6332-6277* • *Open 8am–midnight daily (clubs open till late)* • *www.chijmes.com.sg*

7 The Istana and Sri Temasek

The Istana, which means "palace" in Malay, was built in 1869 as a governor's residence. Situated on a hilltop, it is a blend of traditional Malay palace design and Italian Renaissance decor.

Ⓢ *Map D3, D4* • *Orchard Rd.* • *Open 8:30am–6pm, on select public holidays* • *Adm* • *www.istana.gov.sg*

8 Emerald Hill Road

Pre-war row houses lining this road were some of the earliest to be conserved as private residences. Their architecture illustrates the myriad cultural influences of the 1900s. Houses of note are at numbers 41, 77, and 79–81 (see p91).

9 Tan House

This house, built in 1900, is a mix of cultural influences, with European columns and arched windows, Chinese green tiles above the front portico, and Malay wooden detailing that hangs from the eaves. Ⓢ *Map F4* • *37 Kerbau Rd.* • *No public access*

10 The Esplanade – Theatres on the Bay

Built at a cost of S$600 million, the Esplanade opened in 2002 amid debate over its aesthetic worth. The aluminum shades encasing its domes inspire locals to call it "the Durian," after the spiky local fruit. Ⓢ *Map N2* • *1 Esplanade Drive* • *6828-8377* • *Open 10am–11pm daily* • *www.esplanade.com*

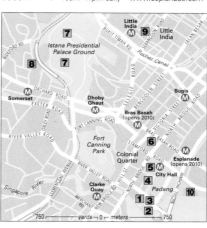

Left **Wedding gifts, Peranakan Museum** Center **Hua Song Museum porcelain** Right **Changi Museum**

🔟 Museums

1 National Museum of Singapore

Singapore's oldest museum is also its best, telling the island's story from the 14th century to the present. The exhibits are interesting for all ages, and history buffs can enjoy eyewitness accounts on the free audio companion (see pp8–9).

2 Asian Civilisations Museum

Housed in Empress Place Building, this museum explores the history, art, and culture of Asia, with 1,300 artifacts that include Islamic art, Indonesian shrines, and textiles. A Singapore River gallery examines the history of the river (see pp10–11).

3 Peranakan Museum

Housed in a wing of the Asian Civilisations Museum, this museum explores the culture of

Breeze by Anthony Poon at Singapore Art Museum

the Peranakans, people born of intermarriage between Chinese traders who settled in Singapore and local women. The resulting culture is seen in bejeweled clothing, furniture, and a diorama depicting a wedding. 🗺 *Map L1*
- *39 Armenian St.* • *6332-7591*
- *Open 1–7pm Mon, 9am–7pm Tue–Sun (9pm Fri)*
- *Adm (half-price adm Fri)* •
www. peranakanmuseum.sg

4 Singapore Art Museum

This building houses the world's largest public collection of modern Southeast Asian art. It combines works from the National Museum with others by contemporary Asian artists. The museum also hosts talks and exhibitions.
🗺 *Map L1, M1* • *71 Bras Basah Rd.*
• *6332-3222* • *Open 10am–7pm daily (9pm Fri)* • *Adm* • *www.singart.com*

5 Malay Heritage Centre

Built as a palace for the Sultan's son, this is now a cultural center for Malays, one of the four ethnic races in Singapore. The galleries explore their history. The center hosts batik and pottery workshops for children and adults.
🗺 *Map H4* • *85 Sultan Gate* • *6391-0450* • *Open 10am–6pm Tue–Sun, 1–6pm Mon* • *Adm* • *www.malayheritage.org.sg*

Malay Heritage Centre

 Most of Singapore's museums are accessible to wheelchair users, but call in advance to confirm.

6 Chinatown Heritage Centre

Dioramas in three shophouses of this center re-create the conditions in which early Chinese immigrants lived. Families were packed into cubicles, and battled poverty, disease, and opium addiction.
Ⓢ Map K4 • 48 Pagoda St. • 6325-2878 • Open 9am–8pm daily • Adm
• www.chinatownheritage.com.sg

A Hindu wedding re-created at Images of Singapore

7 Images of Singapore

This award-winning museum features multimedia displays, starting with a presentation of Raffles' arrival in Singapore and the influx of Chinese, Malay, and Indian immigrants and their impact on the island's culture.
Ⓢ Map S3 • Imbiah Lookout, Sentosa
• 6275-0388 • Open 9am–7pm daily
• Adm • www.sentosa.com.sg

8 Changi Museum

This moving museum commemorates the World War II prisoner-of-war camp for Allied troops and civilians that was housed at Changi Prison. Nearly 5,000 POWs were held here.
Ⓢ Map U2 • 1000 Upper Changi Rd.
• 6214-2451 • Open 9:30am–5pm daily
• www.changimuseum.com

9 Hua Song Museum

Hua Song means "in praise of the Chinese," and this center promotes the impact of Chinese culture on the world. Displays show journeys of early emigrants and their lives working as cooks, porters, and laborers. Ⓢ Map S3
• Haw Par Villa, 262 Pasir Panjang Rd.
• 6339-6833 • Open 10am–6pm Tue–Sun, closed on Mon unless it is a public holiday
• Adm • www.huasong.org

10 Sun Yat Sen Nanyang Memorial Hall

This was the Singapore branch of the Chinese Revolutionary Alliance run by Dr. Sun Yat Sen, the father of the Chinese Revolution. It depicts his life, his conversion to Christianity and his political career (see p98).

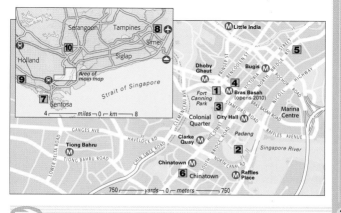

Left **Temple lanterns** Center **Telok Ayer church** Right **Cathedral of the Good Shepherd**

Places of Worship

St. Andrew's Cathedral

Named for the patron saint of Scotland, this Anglican church is on a piece of land selected by Raffles himself. Inside the church is the Canterbury Stone, presented by the Metropolitan Cathedral Church of Canterbury. The Coventry Cross is made of silver-plated nails from the ruins of Coventry Cathedral, and the Coronation Carpet is part of the one used for Queen Elizabeth II in Westminster Abbey (see p34).

Armenian Church

Built in 1835 and dedicated to St. Gregory the Illuminator, this church was the focal point for an Armenian community that has now dwindled to almost nil. Behind the church are grave-stones of prominent community members, such as the Sarkies brothers who founded the Raffles Hotel and the lady for whom the national flower, the Vanda Miss Joaquim, is named. ◈ Map L2 • 60 Hill St. • 6334-0141

Cathedral of the Good Shepherd

Catholicism arrived with the Portuguese in the 1500s. In Singapore's early days, Catholic services were held in a thatched structure at Bras Basah Road. By the mid-1800s this church had been built, along with a school, St. Joseph's Institution, and the Convent of the Holy Infant Jesus, all within close proximity. Non-Catholics are welcome for mass. ◈ Map M1 • 4 Queen St. • 6337-2036 • Open 7am–5pm Mon–Fri, 7am–7:30pm Sat–Sun • www.veritas.org.sg

CHIJMES (Convent of the Holy Infant Jesus)

The Gothic chapel within this complex is Singapore's most ornate church. Although services stopped in 1983, when it became an entertainment complex, the chapel still hosts weddings and receptions. A door in the northeast corner of the grounds is the spot where abandoned babies were left to be cared for by nuns (see p35).

Sri Thandayuthapani Temple

This Hindu temple had humble beginnings as a statue of Lord Muruga under a *bodhi* tree.

St. Andrew's Cathedral

A permanent temple was built in 1859 but was replaced by a new one in 1983. It is renovated every 12 years, in keeping with Hindu tradition. 🕾 Map K1 • 15 Tank Rd. • 6737-9393 • Open 8am–noon, 5:30–8:30pm daily • www.sttemple.com

Tan Si Chong Su Temple

This shrine is dedicated to the Tan family clan. It was originally built on the riverside, but due to land reclamation it now lies well away from the water's edge. Behind the temple, a private hall encloses ancestral tablets of diseased clan members. 🕾 Map K3 • 15 Magazine Rd. • 6533-2880

Lord Muruga at Sri Thandayuthapani Temple

Hong San See Temple

Built on a hill above Mohammed Sultan Road, this 100-year-old temple complex was erected by migrants from the Fujian province in China. Inside the entrance hall are granite plaques listing the donors who contributed to the building. It is dedicated to the God of Fortune, the Goddess of Mercy and the Heavenly Emperor. It was designated as a national monument in 1978. 🕾 Map J2 • 31 Mohammed Sultan Rd.

Maghain Aboth Synagogue

Jews first arrived in Singapore from Iran and Iraq in 1831. Their oldest synagogue in Singapore, Maghain Aboth or "shield of our fathers," was

consecrated in 1878. 🕾 Map L1 • 24 Waterloo St. • 6337-2189 • www.singaporejews.com

Telok Ayer Chinese Methodist Church

Hokkien Methodists built this church in 1924. Many details, such as the windows and arches, are Roman-style while the roofline is distinctly traditional Chinese. Services are held in Chinese, Mandarin, and Hokkien dialects. 🕾 Map L5 • 235 Telok Ayer St. • 6324-4001 • Open 9am–5pm daily • www.tacmc.org.sg

Kong Meng San Phor Kork See Temple

The largest Buddhist temple in Singapore, this 1920 complex was built to house the growing numbers of monks residing in the city. It continues to be an important monastry. The Hall of Great Strength and the Hall of Great Compassion closes at 4:30pm but the compound is open till late. 🕾 Map T2 • 88 Bright Hill Drive • 6849-5300 • Open 6am–9:30pm daily • www.kmspks.org

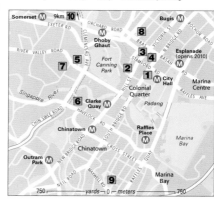

Left **Replica of a British gun, Johore Battery** Right **World War II storyboards, Changi Museum**

World War II Sights

1 Changi Chapel and Museum
This museum is dedicated to prisoners held at Changi Prison and camp from 1942 to 1945, and features replicas of the murals painted in St. Luke's Chapel by Bombardier Stanley Warren *(see p37)*.

2 Fort Siloso
The last British coastal fort on the island offers an insight into the lives of World War II soldiers. The Surrender Chambers re-create the 1945 British and Japanese surrenders *(see pp26–7)*.

Gravestone at Kranji Cemetery

3 Labrador Park
Guns capable of firing shells almost 10 miles (16 km) were installed at Fort Pasir Panjang to help protect it from attack by sea. Many of the gun emplacements can still be seen. ◈ *Map S3 • Labrador Villa Rd. • 6339-6833 • Open 10am–6pm daily • Adm*

4 Battle Box
The British command center during World War II, the Battle Box was designed to be bomb-proof and capable of recycling its air supply. Models depict the 1942 meeting in which General Percival decided to surrender to the Japanese.
◈ *Map E6 • Fort Canning Rise • Open 10am–6pm daily • Adm*

5 Reflections at Bukit Chandu
In February 1942, 1,400 soldiers of the Malay Regiment took a stand on Bukit Chandu against 13,000 Japanese soldiers. This museum recounts the battle and the astonishing courage displayed by the soldiers.
◈ *Map S3 • 31-K Pepys Rd. • 6375-2510 • Open 9am–5pm Tue–Sun • Adm*

6 Johore Battery
The British guns at Johore were the largest outside the UK when they were installed in 1939 for the defence of Singapore. The originals were destroyed before the fall of Singapore but those have now been replaced with replicas. Tunnels used to store ammunition were discovered here in 1991 by the Singapore Prisons Department.
◈ *Map V2 • Cotsford Rd. • 6546-9897 • Open 9am–5pm daily*

Re-construction of a war-time meeting at Battle Box

Civilian War Memorial

Kranji War Memorial and Cemetery
This memorial stands over the graves of more than 4,000 Allied servicemen. The pillars list the names of 24,000 others whose bodies were not found *(see p99)*.

Civilian War Memorial
Locally known as the "chop-sticks memorial," the four pillars symbolize the races (Chinese, Malay, Indian, and others) that suffered during the Japanese occupation. Remains of unidentified victims are buried at the base of the monument.
⬡ *Map M2 • War Memorial, Beach Rd.*

The Padang
The spot where Japanese troops gathered and divided the European population. British and Australian soldiers were to be held at the Seralang Barracks, while 2,300 civilians were sent to Changi Prison *(see pp22–3)*.

Lim Bo Seng Memorial
This monument is a tribute to local hero Lim Bo Seng, who escaped to Sri Lanka after the Japanese invasion to train resistance fighters. Captured upon his return, he died in captivity.
⬡ *Map M3 • Queen Elizabeth Walk*

Major World War II Events in Singapore

December 7–8, 1941
The Japanese attack Pearl Harbor and simultaneously launch a massive offensive, invading the Philippines, Hong Kong, and Thailand, and drop the first bombs on Singapore.

February 8, 1942
Japan invades Singapore from Malaysia, by crossing the causeway.

February 15, 1942
General Percival surrenders to General Yamashito. The Japanese occupation begins.

February 16, 1942
The European population assembles at the Padang, before being marched 14 miles (23 km) to Changi Prison.

May 1943
The first group of 600 prisoners is dispatched to work on the Burma-Thailand "death railway."

1943
Rations are cut as the war turns against Japan and living conditions begin to worsen.

November 1944
Starvation and disease is widespread. The US carries out its first raid on the Singapore harbor.

Early 1945
Living conditions are almost unbearable, with many people dying of malnutrition.

May 1945
News of the end of the European War reaches Singapore – the end is near for the desperate city.

September 12, 1945
Japan formally surrenders to Lord Louis Mountbatten, the last British Viceroy to India.

Left **Beach at East Coast Park** Right **Boardwalk at Sungei Buloh Wetland Reserve**

🔟 National Parks and Gardens

1 Singapore Botanic Gardens

Although Orchard Road is just a short walk away, the city seems deceptively distant when you are surrounded by frangipani trees, lakes, and rain forest. A walk through the tranquil gardens is the perfect follow-up to a day of sightseeing or shopping. Locals may be seen practicing the martial art Tai Chi on the lawns in the morning (see pp18–19).

Monkey at Bukit Timah Nature Reserve

2 National Orchid Garden

One of the highlights of the Botanic Gardens is this collection of over 3,000 species of orchid. Beautifully landscaped, the garden boasts different environments for each group of orchids and bromeliads. The Coolhouse provides a welcome respite from the heat (see pp18-19).

3 Fort Canning Park

This park is inextricably linked with every era of Singapore's history. Originally called "Forbidden Hill," it is said to be the site of the tomb of Iskandar Shah, who first settled Singapore. Raffles built his bungalow here but, in 1859, it was replaced by a military base and renamed Fort Canning. The fort became the British headquarters in the Battle for Singapore. Raffles designated it the island's first botanic garden (see p85).

4 Chinese and Japanese Gardens

Two unique landscaping philosophies have been used to create two gardens on adjoining islands on Jurong Lake. The Chinese Garden features an excellent Suzhou-style bonsai collection, colorful buildings, and a stone boat. Steps away over the Bridge of Double Beauty, the Japanese Garden is the essence of serenity. Enjoy the view of both from the top of the Chinese Garden's seven-story pagoda (see p97).

The serene Chinese and Japanese Gardens

5 Bukit Timah Nature Reserve

One of the last remnants of Singapore's primary rain forest, Bukit Timah is thought to hold more plant species than all of North America. Expect to see long-tailed macaques and flying lemurs. Routes around the reserve range from 45-minute walks to 2-hour hikes and mountain biking trails *(see p97)*.

Full bloom at the National Orchid Garden

6 MacRitchie Nature Trail

Vestiges of Singapore's rubber plantations can be seen from the boardwalk encircling this reservoir park. Trails through the forest range in length from 2 to 7 miles (3 to 11 km). The 82-ft (25-m)-high treetop walk has views of the forest canopy and the reservoir. ⓢ *Map S2 • Off Lornie Rd. • Open daily • www.nparks.gov.sg*

7 Sungei Buloh Wetland Reserve

Boardwalk trails wind through this reserve among mangroves that are home to mudskippers and monitor lizards. Look out for the Atlas moth, one of the largest in the world, with a wing-span of up to 1 ft (12 inches). Hides by the pools allow you to observe some of the 144 bird species found here *(see p98)*.

8 East Coast Park

For many visitors, this park is their first glimpse of Singapore, stretching along the expressway from the airport to the city. The long strip of sandy beach with paths shaded by casuarina trees and coconut palms is popular with bicyclists and roller-bladers. From here the countless ships plying the Strait make for an incongruous sight. ⓢ *Map T3 • East Coast Parkway • Open 7am–7pm daily • www.nparks.gov.sg*

9 Chek Jawa

This marine preserve has a boardwalk over the shore, from where you can spot horseshoe crabs, starfish, anemones, and sponges. Visits must be arranged in advance. ⓢ *Map V1 • Eastern tip of Pulau Ubin • 6542-4108 • www.nparks.gov.sg*

10 Sentosa Nature Walk

Given its short distance and well-graded paths, this walk is one of the easiest ways for children or less able visitors to glimpse Singapore's forest. However, it is not accessible for strollers and wheelchairs *(see pp26–7)*.

Left **Procession during Thaipusam** Right **Annual Chingay Parade**

Religious Celebrations

Chinese New Year
Singapore's most important public holiday is celebrated in January or February. Celebrations begin on the eve of the holiday, with families gathering for dinner. People visit their friends and family, and *hong bao* (red packets containing money) are given to elders and kids.

Chingay Parade
This Chinese New Year parade features performances of dance, music, and acrobatics as well as floats along the route. Troupes from China and performers from all over the world add a multicultural aspect to the event.

Hungry Ghost Festival offering

Thaipusam
In January or February, this day of thanksgiving sees Hindus honor Lord Muruga. A parade begins at Sri Srinivasa Perumal Temple *(see p75)* and ends at Sri Thandayuthapani Temple *(see pp38–9)*. Many devotees carry heavy *kavadis* (metal racks with fruits and flowers), pierce their tongues and cheeks with skewers, and dig hooks into their backs.

Hungry Ghost Festival
The Chinese believe that menacing spirits wander the earth in August and September. To appease these spirits, they offer food, burn joss sticks and "hell money," and stage Chinese operas. New ventures, such as marriages and business openings, are suspended during this inauspicious time.

Mid-Autumn Festival
Also called the Lantern Festival, this celebrates the harvest with mooncakes stuffed with sweet lotus paste, egg, and other fillings. The Chinese and Japanese Gardens *(see p42)* are a wonderland for kids, with huge paper and plastic lanterns.

Hari Raya Puasa
Ramadan, the Muslim month of fasting, culminates with Hari Raya Puasa, also called Aidil Fitri, and is celebrated with family and friends. Non-Muslims are often invited to feasts in private homes. The dates for this public holiday change every year.

Family celebrating Hari Raya Puasa

7 Thimithi

Every October or November, a procession of Hindu devotees makes its way from the Sri Srinivasa Perumal Temple to the Sri Mariamman Temple *(see p67)* where a fire-walking ceremony is led by priests.

Offerings at a family altar during Deepavali

8 Deepavali

Also held in October or November, this festival is celebrated by Hindus and Sikhs to mark the triumph of good over evil. Hundreds of oil lamps are lit to guide the souls of the departed, who come to earth on this day, back to the afterworld.

9 Nine Emperor Gods

Taoists believe that the Nine Emperor Gods come to earth for nine days each November to care for the sick and bring luck to the living. Priests in Chinese temples chant prayers, and spirit guides write charms in their own blood.

10 Christmas

Singapore keeps the Christmas spirit alive with spectacular decorations on Orchard Road *(see pp90–91)*, which attracts almost a million tourists during the colorful festive season.

Top 10 Sporting and Cultural Events

1 Formula 1 SingTel Singapore Grand Prix

Held in September, this is the first night-time race in Grand Prix history and Asia's first to be held on city streets.

2 Singapore Arts Festival

This month-long festival in June features performing arts groups from around the world.

3 World Gourmet Summit

April sees Singapore host a festival of fine dining, with international celebrity chefs.

4 Singapore International Film Festival

Every April, some 300 art-house and independent films are shown, with a special focus on Asian cinema.

5 Dragon Boat Festival

International teams gather each June to race dragon boats.

6 Singapore Food Festival

This month-long celebration of local food, including tours and classes, is held every July.

7 Great Singapore Sale

For six weeks in June and July, local retailers offer discounts.

8 Ballet Under the Stars

This casual event is held at various outdoor venues across the city every July.

9 National Day, August 9

A huge show marks the day Singapore became a nation. Tickets are available via a lottery.

10 ARTSingapore

Every October, hundreds of Asia's fine art galleries put their best works on sale.

Left **The Substation** Center **Jubilee Theatre** Right **DBS Arts Centre**

Arts Venues

1 The Esplanade – Theatres on the Bay
This iconic landmark of Singapore, built as a center for the performing arts, houses two indoor stages (a concert hall and a smaller recital studio) for music, theater, and dance performances by international and local groups. There is also an outdoor stage located beside Marina Bay (see p35).

2 Victoria Theatre and Concert Hall
Though home to the Singapore Symphony Orchestra, this concert hall stages other performances as well. While acoustically not as strong as the concert hall at The Esplanade, its ambience is superb. The well-preserved original decorative molding, wall sconces, and chandeliers of this ornate Victorian building are as much a part of the performance as the music itself (see p85).

3 The Arts House at Old Parliament House
Rooms formerly used for parliamentary discussions now welcome music and dance performances, poetry readings, lectures, screenings, and other fringe events. The old rooms are intimate, with hardwood floors, decorative molding, and special fixtures, all intact. The building also has a café and pub. (see pp10–11).

4 Jubilee Theatre
Part of the Raffles Hotel's shopping and entertainment annex, this small theater stages independent productions, stand-up comedy, and music performances. A good choice for an evening of drinks, dinner, and a show. Map M1 • Raffles Hotel Arcade • 6337-1886
• www.singapore.raffles.com

5 DBS Arts Centre
Home to the award-winning Singapore Repertory Theatre (SRT) – one of Asia's leading English language repertory theaters and Singapore's most popular troupe – DBS is located amid dining and nightlife venues. The Little Company also hosts performances for children here. Map J2
• 20 Merbau Rd., Robertson Quay • 6733-0005
• www.srt.com.sg

The Esplanade – Theatres on the Bay lobby performance

Art of Our Time Gallery at the Singapore Art Museum

Singapore Art Museum
This museum has the world's largest permanent collection of 20th-century Southeast Asian art held by a public institution. In 1996, it was renovated and fitted with climate-control features to help preserve the exhibits, which include international works on loan *(see p36)*.

MICA Galleries
Clustered in the lobby of the Ministry of Information Communications and the Arts (MICA) building, a group of private art galleries sells contemporary works from Asia's hottest artists, primarily from India, China, and Southeast Asia. Notable galleries include Art-2 and Gajah Gallery. ✪ *Map L2 • 140 Hill St. • Open 11am–7pm daily*

The Substation
Singapore's first home to independent artists has a black box theater, a gallery, and multipurpose rooms. These host diverse events such as indie gigs, traditional dance, poetry readings, experimental theater, and film festivals. ✪ *Map L1 • 45 Armenian St. • 6337-7800 • www.substation.org*

Singapore Tyler Print Institute
Established in 2002, this institute works with international artists to create outstanding edition prints on paper and to explore the technical and creative aspects of print and paper-making. The institute is housed in a 19th-century warehouse where artists can create, exhibit, and sell their work. ✪ *Map J2 • 41 Robertson Quay • 6336-3663 • Open 10am–6pm Mon–Sat • www.stpi.com.sg*

Sculpture Square
This gallery, on the site of an 1875 church, is dedicated to contemporary 3D art by local and regional artists. Community programs are held throughout the year to promote art locally. ✪ *Map F5 • 1 Middle Rd. • 6333-1055 • Open 11am–6pm Mon–Fri, noon–6pm Sat–Sun • www.sculpturesq.com.sg*

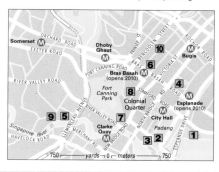

Left **VivoCity** Right **Challenger store at Funan DigitaLife Mall**

TOP 10 Shopping Malls

1 VivoCity

Singapore's biggest mall also has some of its best views, with platforms overlooking the cable cars swinging over to Sentosa. VivoCity is well-designed and airy with great facilities, including a multiplex cinema, food courts and restaurants, a children's playground, and even a rooftop wading pool.
❍ Map S3 • 1 HarbourFront Walk • 6377-6870 • Open 10am–10pm daily

2 Ngee Ann City

This marble monolith is often known by the name of its main tenant, Takashimaya. The Japanese store rubs shoulders with luxury names, such as Louis Vuitton, Chanel, and Tiffany. Fashion clothing chains include Zara, Mango, and Giordano. The food court is good. Bibliophiles must not miss Kinokuniya Singapore, which claims to be Asia's largest bookstore *(see p92)*.

3 Tanglin Shopping Centre

Not to be confused with Tanglin Mall, this place is a chance to escape familiar global brands and browse antiques, jewelry, and art in a relaxed atmosphere. There is a fine selection of traditional and modern Asian furniture and carpets – Hassan's is one of Singapore's oldest family-run carpet businesses. Select Books is a bookstore specializing in Southeast Asian titles. ❍ Map A4 • 19 Tanglin Rd. • 6737-0849 • Open noon–6pm Mon–Sat

Buddha statue in Tanglin Shopping Centre

4 Shopping Gallery at Hilton

Exclusivity is the game at glamorous Hilton arcade. Browse three floors of designer boutiques including Missoni, Gucci, and Valentino before taking the link bridge to the Four Seasons Hotel arcade to enjoy its choice of art and paintings. ❍ Map A4 • 581 Orchard Rd. • 6734-5250

Ngee Ann City Mall on Orchard Road

Most malls get very crowded on weekends, when Singaporean families go to shop, eat, and escape the heat.

The entrance to Lucky Plaza

Far East Plaza

There are more than 800 stores in this bustling complex. The Plaza is crowded and shabby but presents a different side of Orchard Road. Lower floors specialize in street fashion and local designers; upstairs are tailors, hairdressers, and tattoo parlors. ◈ *Map B4 • 330 Orchard Rd. • 6734-2325 • Open 11am–10pm daily*

Lucky Plaza

On Sundays, the city's army of foreign domestic workers congregates here, since the mall is a gathering place for the local Filipino community. Check products and charges carefully, because Lucky Plaza has a reputation for sharp operators. ◈ *Map B4 • 304 Orchard Rd. • 6235-3294 • Open 10am–9pm daily*

Sim Lim Square

Six floors of gadgets make Sim Lim a technophile's idea of heaven. As Singapore's biggest electronics mall, it has a huge choice of products. Ensure that you buy only from an authorized dealer and that voltage requirements of electronic goods are adaptable to your home country. ◈ *Map F4 • 1 Rochor Canal Rd. • 6338-3859 • Open 10:30am–9pm daily*

Funan DigitaLife Mall

Fair prices, reputable stores, a peaceful atmosphere, and genuine products make Funan a good place to buy electronics. An on-site Cash Refund Counter enables tourists to get an instant refund on Goods & Service Tax *(see p109)*. ◈ *Map L2 • 109 North Bridge Rd. • 6336-8327 • Open 10:30am–8:30pm daily*

Raffles City Shopping Centre

This center of interlinking malls joins the Stamford and Fairmont hotels with City Hall MRT, the CityLink, and Marina Square. The concierge service here can book tours and events, and provide strollers and wheelchairs. ◈ *Map M2 • 252 North Bridge Rd. • 6318-0238 • Open 10am–9:30pm daily*

Singapore Handicraft Centre

This center brings together 50 independent stores, which offer everything from souvenirs to Chinese antiques, jade, and art. Many local artists and photographers sell their pictures here. ◈ *Map K3 • 133 New Bridge Rd. • 6534-0112 • Open 10:30am–6pm daily*

Left **Wild Wild Wet water park** Center **Singapore Science Centre** Right **Escape Theme Park**

Children's Activities

1 Escape Theme Park
Enjoy this park's roller coaster, Ferris wheel, and Asia's tallest flume ride. The Inverter is for older kids while the Red Baron flyer is for younger ones. ⊛ *Map U2 • 1 Pasir Ris Close • 6581-9128 • Open 10am–8pm Sat & Sun (daily during school vacations) • Adm • www.escapethemepark.com*

2 Wild Wild Wet
Get soaked on the flumes, water mazes, and Ular-Lah – Southeast Asia's first white-water-rafting slide. ⊛ *Map U2 • 1 Pasir Ris Close • 6581-9128 • Open 1–7pm Mon & Wed–Fri, 10am–7pm weekends & public holidays • Adm • www.wildwildwet.com*

3 eXplorerKid Family Park
While little ones work their way through the obstacles of the Mystical Forest, parents can work out or enjoy DVDs in the grown-ups zone. ⊛ *Map U2 • 1 Pasir Ris Close • 6589-1668 • Open noon–10pm Mon–Thu (off-peak), 10am–10pm Fri–Sun & public holidays • Adm • www.explorerkid.com*

4 Singapore Science Centre
Its 850 exhibits are enough to attract any child. Sculptures in the Kinetic Garden showcase wind, water, and solar power. The Discovery Zone has an insectarium with creepy crawlies. ⊛ *Map R2 • 15 Science Centre Rd. • 6425-2500 • Open 10am–6pm Tue–Sun • Adm • www.science.edu.sg*

Resident macaws at Jurong BirdPark

5 Singapore Discovery Centre
Discover contemporary Singapore at this "edutainment" center, with a Giant Light and Sound Show to enthrall you and a Smart Show to test you on subjects ranging from math to music. ⊛ *Map Q2 • 510 Upper Jurong Rd. • 6792-6188 • Open 9am–6pm Tue–Sun • Adm • www.sdc.com.sg*

6 Underwater World
Sharks and rays glide overhead as a travelator carries visitors through an aquarium tunnel. Children can help feed endangered turtles or be hands on with starfish, rays, and baby sharks in the shallow touch pool (see p26).

The fascinating Underwater World

A dolphin encounter at the Dolphin Lagoon

Jurong BirdPark
This is one of the largest parks of its kind. An overhead railroad runs through the Waterfall Aviary, featuring the world's tallest man-made waterfall *(see p97)*.

Singapore Crocodile Farm
Learn about crocodiles and see how many species you can spot from the shady paths at this historic breeding farm. The 1940s skinning factory is preserved in its original state. ⊗ *Map T2 • 790 Upper Serangoon Rd. • 6288-9385 • Open 9am–6pm daily, ¢ public holidays • www.singaporecrocfarm.com*

Snow City
Board or ski at Snow City, while children build snowmen or check out the igloo in the play area. The temperature is maintained at 23°F (-5°C) so dress warmly. Coats and boots can be rented. ⊗ *Map R2 • 21 Jurong Town Hall Rd. • 6560-2306 • Open 9:45am–5:15pm Tue–Sun • Adm • www.snowcity.com.sg*

Dolphin Lagoon
Children will love to watch Indo-Pacific Humpback dolphins leap, spin, and play. Lucky visitors get to feed and swim with the dolphins in pre-booked sessions. ⊗ *Map S3 • Palawan Beach, Sentosa • 6275-0030 • Open 10:30am–6pm daily • Adm • www.sentosa.com.sg*

Top 10 Sports

1 Golf
Courses at Marina Bay, Sentosa *(see pp26–7)*, and Tanah Merah are open to visitors. ⊗ *Map V2 • Tanah Merah Country Club, 25 Changi Coast Rd. • 6545-1731*

2 Sea Canoeing
Kayaks and canoes can be rented in Sentosa or at East Coast Park *(see p43)*.

3 Water-skiing
SKI360, Singapore's first cable-ski park, tows skiers and wakeboarders around a cableway. ⊗ *Map U2 • 1206A East Coast Parkway • 6442-7318*

4 Windsurfing
Water-Venture at East Coast Park offers watersports instruction and equipment. ⊗ *Map T3 • 1390 East Coast Parkway • 6444-0409*

5 Sailing
The Singapore Sailing Federation runs courses for all ages. ⊗ *Map U2 • 1500 East Coast Parkway • 6444-4555*

6 Scuba Diving
Several companies offer training, equipment, and arrange trips to good diving spots. ⊗ *Map R2 • Diventures, S-17 Pandan Loop • 6778-0661*

7 Hiking
Hike through rain forest parks at Bukit Timah and MacRitchie *(see pp42–3)*.

8 Biking
Bicycles can be rented at East Coast Park, Sentosa, and Pulau Ubin *(see pp42–3)*.

9 Rollerblading
East Coast Park is superb for rollerblading, and has many rental shops.

10 Beach Volleyball
Siloso Beach on Sentosa has four popular courts, so go early at weekends.

Left **Oriental Spa** Center **Shirodhara oil treatment at Ayurlly Ayurvedic Spa** Right **Spa Botanica**

^{TOP}10 Spas

1 Willow Stream Spa

This spa is a haven of earth tones. For a full body pampering, try the Willow Stream Elements, with a moor mud wrap, aromatherapy, mineral bath, and a warm massage. The Singapore Luxury Facial is a divine experience including a hand, foot, and scalp massage. ◈ *Map M1*
• *Fairmont Singapore, 80 Bras Basah Rd.*
• *6431-5600 • Open 9am–10pm daily*
• *www.fairmont.com*

2 Spa Esprit at HOUSE

After a long, cramped flight, head here for a Kajogal massage. A therapist will gently stretch your limbs into 20 different yoga positions. Emerge loose and ready for a drink at the in-house bar, Camp, or the Tippling Club. ◈ *Map S3 • 8D Dempsey Rd. • 6479-0070 • Open 10am–9pm daily, till 1am Thu–Sat • www.dempseyhouse.com*

3 Estheva Spa

This ladies-only spa is all about luxury. Try the "choc de-ager" treatment, which consists of a chocolate body

Estheva Spa

An Aspara suite

scrub, a chocolate fondue wrap and warm almond oil massage. These treatments combined are said to have four times the antioxidants of tea. ◈ *Map A4 • Palais Renaissance, 390 Orchard Rd. • 6733-9300 • Open 10am–10pm Mon–Fri, 10am–8pm Sat–Sun • www.estheva.com*

4 The Asian Spa

With therapists from Japan, Singapore, and Thailand, this spa combines a range of Asian and Western treatments. Indulge in a traditional Javanese massage followed by a collagen facial. Signature treatments include the Aroma Meridian massage, which combines Chinese yin and yang, and uses both Western aromatherapy and acupressure. ◈ *Map M3 • Fullerton Hotel, 1 Fullerton Square • 6877-8183 • Open 10am–11pm daily*

5 The Aspara

Therapists at the Aspara are trained in Swedish, Thai, and Indonesian massage techniques. Aromatherapy massage is the specialty and the treatment uses

custom-blended massage oils and sugar scrubs. ◈ *Map B3*
• *Goodwood Park Hotel, 22 Scotts Rd.* • *6732-3933*
• *Open 10am–11pm daily*

6 Ayurlly Ayurvedic Spa

The outdoor pool at Spaboutique

Centuries-old Ayurvedic holistic techniques are used at this spa, where herbal medicated oils are custom-blended after a thorough and detailed diagnostic interview. The *Chandramukhi*, a synchronized massage by two therapists, promises to treat rheumatism, poor eyesight, sleep problems, and even increase life span. ◈ *Map F4* • *Tekka Mall, 2 Serangoon Rd.* • *6737-5657* • *Open 10am–8pm Mon–Sat* • *www.mayooryspa.com*

7 The Oriental Spa

Tranquillity descends as you step into this spa to enjoy an Oriental Massage combining Thai, Swedish, and Shiatsu techniques. There is also a Couple's Suite with a private relaxation area. ◈ *Map N2* • *Mandarin Oriental Singapore, 5 Raffles Avenue* • *6338-0066* • *www.mandarinoriental.com*

8 Spa Botanica

This spa is located in lush gardens with mud-pools and waterfalls. Its award-winning treatments include the 3-hour Singapore Flower Ritual – a deep-pressure outdoor massage followed by aromatherapy and a bath with frangipani blossoms. ◈ *Map S3*
• *Sentosa Resort and Spa, 2 Bukit Manis Rd.* • *6371-1318*
• *Open 10am–10pm daily*
• *www.spabotanica.com*

9 Spaboutique

Based in a colonial-era black-and-white bungalow, this spa is filled with antiques and art, and has a beautiful garden. All the treatments are of an extremely high standard, but the Rose and Lavender Scrub Wrap, which makes the skin glow, is almost miraculous. ◈ *Map S3*
• *6 Nassim Rd.* • *6887-0760* • *Open noon–10pm Mon–Fri, 10:30am–10pm Sat–Sun* • *www.spaboutique.com.sg*

10 Bel Amis SPA de Feng

Open only to men, this spa's most popular treatment is the Spa de Feng Relaxation Massage that offers a balance of Swedish, Japanese Shiatsu, and Chinese Acupressure. The Detoxification Massage is specially designed to encourage lymphatic drainage.
◈ *Map L3* • *18B Circular Rd.* • *6533-5076*
• *Open 11am–10pm Mon–Thu, noon–11pm Fri–Sun* • *www.spadefeng.com*

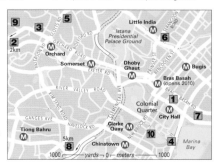

Left **A foodstall at Maxwell** Center **Newton Food Centre** Right **Food Republic at Wisma Atria**

🖭 **Hawker Centers and Food Courts**

1 Maxwell Food Centre

A Chinatown favorite, this hawker center has an extensive menu of Chinese favorites, served with rice. Try the famous Hainanese chicken at Tian Tian Hainanese Chicken Rice stall. 🆂 *Map K5 • Corner of South Bridge Rd. & Maxwell Rd. • Open 11am–10pm daily*

2 Lau Pa Sat Festival Market

Located in the heart of the financial district, this Victorian market is quite popular

Local chili crab

with the lunchtime crowd. It also hops late at night, when crowds come for satay and barbecued stingray served with beer. 🆂 *Map M4 • Corner of Cross St. & Raffles Quay • Open 11am–3am daily*

3 Newton Food Centre

Open round-the-clock, Newton is busiest early in the morning. It is a favorite place for tour guides, too. Order carefully from seafood stalls, which are known to overcharge foreigners. Try fish ball noodles at Soon Wah. 🆂 *Map C2 • 500 Clemenceau Ave. • Open 11am–3am daily*

4 Chomp Chomp

A famous suburban hawker center, Chomp Chomp serves excellent barbecued seafood in its relaxed garden setting. There is a good fried carrot cake stall, too. 🆂 *Map T2 • 20 Kensington Park • Open 11am–3am daily*

5 East Coast Lagoon Food Village

Ocean breezes keep eating areas cool at this center beside the sea. Find good barbecued seafood at Leng Heng, *laksa* at Roxy, and satay at Haron 30. Enjoy a beer on the beach after your meal. 🆂 *Map U2 • 1220 East Coast Park Service Rd. • Open 11am–11pm daily*

6 Tekka Market

This popular hawker center has moved temporarily while its old haunt undergoes renovation. Despite its Little India location, you can find good examples of every cuisine here including, of course, Indian. 🆂 *Map F3 • Temporary address: Race Course Rd. • Open 11am–11pm daily*

Food hall at Lau Pa Sat Festival Market

Alfresco dining on Chinatown Food Street

Food Republic
This mall food court combines excellent hawker stalls with restaurants offering terrific variety. Outlets are decorated in Asian marketplace-style. ⓦ *Wisma Atria: Map B4 • 435 Orchard Rd.* ⓦ *Suntec City Mall: Map P2 • Temasek Ave.* ⓦ *VivoCity: see p48*

Chinatown Complex
Freshly renovated, this hawker center is known for the best and most authentic Chinese food in Singapore. Try everything from *cze cha* to local-style carrot cake, claypot rice, and dumplings. ⓦ *Map K4 • Block 335 Smith St. • Open 11am–11pm daily*

Chinatown Food Street
At 6pm, this street closes to vehicular traffic and tables are set up. Diners can order food from any stall and have it delivered to their table. Boon Tat Street Barbecued Seafood is especially good. ⓦ *Map K6 • Smith St. • Open 6–11pm daily*

Makansutra Glutton's Bay
Great for late-night snacking, this waterfront hawker center serves *mee goreng* (spicy fried noodles), barbecued chicken wings, and cold beer. ⓦ *Map N2 • 8 Raffles Avenue • Open 6pm–3am daily*

Top 10 Local Dishes

Laksa
Rice noodles, prawns, and fishcakes in a rich soup made from coconut curry, topped with chili and laksa leaf – a local herb.

Kaya Toast
A sweet jam made from coconut milk and egg, which is spread on toast and eaten for breakfast or as a snack.

Chili Crab
Whole crab smothered in a sweet and sour, spicy sauce, served with buns for dipping in the sauce.

Fish Head Curry
An entire fish head stewed in spicy curry – the cheek meat is said to be the sweetest.

Banana Leaf
Southern Indian meal of white rice, vegetable curries, and relish served on a flat banana leaf.

Nasi Padang
Indonesian or Malay cooked dishes, such as beef *rendang* or *assam* curry, served over white rice.

Satay
Small skewers of barbecued meats dipped in sweet peanut and chili sauce.

Chicken Rice
Poached or roasted, chopped chicken served over rice cooked in savory chicken stock.

Roti Prata
Indian fried bread, sometimes stuffed with onions, potatoes, or egg, and dipped in *dal* or fish curry.

Chendol
Indonesian dessert made of green jelly noodles, sweet beans, brown sugar, coconut milk, and shaved ice.

Left **Fine dining at the Summer Pavilion** Right **Dining area at Club Chinois**

🔟 Restaurants

1 Raffles Grill

Raffles' most formal and elegant dining room serves distinctly haute French cuisine. The menu changes every season, but past favorites have included melting duck *foie gras*, the freshest roast turbot, and tender *wagyu* beef. The wine list features vintages dating back to 1900. ⊗ *Map M1 • Raffles Hotel, 1 Beach Rd. • 6331-1612 • Open noon–2pm Mon–Fri, 7–10pm Mon–Sat • www.raffles hotel.com • $$$$$*

2 Doc Cheng's

The quirky decor here is a mix of oriental and colonial; even the silverware doubles as chopsticks. Doc Cheng's modern Asian menu showcases flavors from across the continent – wok-fried sweet potato leaves with spicy shrimp paste, *miso* cod, and roasted salmon with Indian spices. ⊗ *Map M1 • Raffles Hotel Arcade, 1 Beach Rd. • 6412-1816 • Open noon–2pm Mon–Fri, 7–10pm daily • $$$$*

Doc Cheng's

3 IndoChine Waterfront

Of the five IndoChine outlets in Singapore, this has the best location. Reserve a table on the terrace overlooking Boat Quay. The food is well-executed Asian fusion, with an emphasis on Vietnamese dishes redolent with lime, chilies, and fresh herbs.
⊗ *Map M3 • 1 Empress Place • 6339-1720 • Open noon–3pm Mon–Fri, 6:30–11:30pm/12:30am daily • www.indochine.com. sg • $$$$*

IndoChine sign

4 Morton's of Chicago

Ebullient waiters at this upmarket steakhouse follow the menu with an immense platter, heaving with sample cuts of beef or vegetables. The seafood competes with superbly fresh lobsters, oysters, and shrimp.
⊗ *Map N2 • Mandarin Oriental Hotel, 5 Raffles Avenue • 6339-3740 • Open 5:30–10/11pm daily • Reservations advisable • www.mortons.com • $$$$$*

5 Club Chinois

Exquisite Cantonese food is served in an opulent dining room here. The Crispy Beijing Duck with five-spiced *foie gras* is delicious, and the roast rack of lamb wonderfully tender. The à la carte menu is fairly pricey, but there is also a range of set menus. ⊗ *Map A4 • Orchard Parade Hotel, 1 Tanglin Rd. • 6834-0660 • Open noon–2:30pm, 6:30–10:30pm daily • www.tunglok.com • $$$$*

Most menus add "++" to their prices indicating that a 10 percent service charge and 8 percent tax will be added to the bill.

6 Summer Pavilion
The Ritz-Carlton's swankiest restaurant serves top-class Cantonese food. The *dim sum* and lobster noodles are quite popular. Set lunches are good value and the service is superb.
◈ Map N2 • 7 Raffles Avenue • 6434-5286 • Open 11:30am–2:30pm and 6:30–10:30pm daily • www.ritzcarlton.com • $$$$$

Morton's of Chicago

7 Au Jardin
Set in the Botanic Gardens, Au Jardin exudes romance. Chef Galvin Lim serves gastronomic French cuisine, offering Table d'Hote and Degustation menus, with a Provencal buffet on Sundays and a menu for Ladies who Lunch on Fridays. ◈ Map S2 • Cluny Rd. • 6466-8812 • Open noon–2pm Fri & Sun, 7pm–late daily • $$$$$

8 Rang Mahal
Food at this luxurious place deserves its regular awards. Try the *thali* (platter) – a selection of soup, appetizers, and dishes from the à la carte menu. There are semi-private areas and a private dining room. ◈ Map N2 • Pan Pacific, 7 Raffles Boulevard • 6333-1788 • Open noon–2:30pm Sun–Fri, 6:30–10:30pm daily • www.rangmahal.com.sg • $$$$

9 Inagiku
A haven of dark earth tones and spot-lighting, Inagiku serves Japanese food. Try affordable set lunches of lobster and beef tenderloin or the exquisite sushi.
◈ Map M1 • Fairmont Singapore, 80 Bras Basah Rd. • 6431-6156 • Open noon–2:30pm and 6:30–10:30pm daily • www.fairmont.com • $$$$$

10 Pierside Kitchen and Bar
Excellent seafood is the focus here. Along the waterfront, diners sit in rope chairs shaded by canvas sails. Try the fresh *fruit de mer*, vanilla poached lobster or octopus, or vine-ripened tomato salad. ◈ Map M3 • 1 Fullerton Rd. • 6348-0400 • Open 11:30am–2:30pm and 6:30–10:30pm Mon–Thu, 6:30–11pm Fri–Sat • www.marmaladegroup.com • $$$$

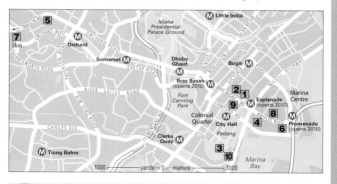

For a key to price categories see pp71, 83, 89, 95, 101

Left **Harry's Bar, Boat Quay** Right **The Café del Mar poolside**

🔟 Bars and Lounges

1 Harry's Bar, Boat Quay
This place is famous as rogue trader Nick Leeson's old watering hole. Its position next to the financial district ensures it is still a favorite with financiers for after-work drinks and food. It has riverside alfresco seating, and live jazz and blues from the house band and visiting artists.
⊗ *Map L3 • 28 Boat Quay • 6538-3029*
• Open 11am–1am Sun–Thu, 11am–2am Fri–Sat

2 Harry's, Dempsey Hill
The Harry's chain recently added this unpretentious, relaxed lounge in a growing community of galleries, restaurants, and pubs on Dempsey Hill. It is a laid-back place with sofas and low tables. Happy hour runs from 5pm to 9pm and there's live evening music from Wednesday to Saturday. ⊗ *Map S3 • Block 11, Dempsey Rd. • 6471-9019 • Open 4pm–1 or 2am Mon–Fri, noon–1 or 2am Sat–Sun*

3 Crazy Elephant
Local and visiting musicians play rock 'n' roll here every night. With a focus on music and beer, Crazy Elephant is a more casual option than many fashionable bars in the area. There is outside seating overlooking the river.
⊗ *Map K2 • Clarke Quay • 6337-7859*
• Open 5pm–2 or 3am daily

4 No. 5, Emerald Hill
In a restored 1910 Peranakan shophouse just off Orchard Road, No. 5's location, cocktail list, and buzzy ambience appeal to the expatriate crowd after work. During the day it's quieter and easier to admire the Chinese teak carving and opium beds at the back. ⊗ *Map C5 • 5 Emerald Hill • 6732-0818 • Open noon–2 or 3am daily*

5 Jazz@Southbridge
The owner of this crowded, buzzy bar is a purist. No blues or rock music is permitted to dilute

Live music at the Crazy Elephant

the top-class jazz. There is a great house band and excellent guest performers, with jam nights on Sunday evenings. A dedicated Whisky Bar offers over 60 varieties of malts and blends. ◈ *Map L3 • 82b Boat Quay • 6327-4671 • Open 5:30pm–1am Tue–Sun (until 2am Fri–Sat)*

Café del Mar Singapore

Head over to Sentosa's Siloso Beach to grab a lounge chair by the pool and enjoy the sunset at this Ibiza-style beach club. DJs play jazz-club fusion during the day, and caipirinhas and piña coladas help the party along. The relaxed atmosphere turns energetic on Saturdays when the club hosts foam parties. ◈ *Map S3 • 40 Siloso Beach Walk, Sentosa • 6235-1296 • Open 11am–1am Mon–Fri, 24 hrs at weekends*

Muddy Murphy's Irish Pub

When the urge for a Guinness is irresistible, this friendly pub delivers more than most shamrock-themed bars. Despite a basement address, it offers a welcome outdoor seating area. Inside, a big-screen TV shows rugby and soccer internationals. There is live pop and rock music on weekends. ◈ *Map A3 • 442 Orchard Rd. • 6735-0400 • Open 11am–1 or 2am daily*

Loof

With a blend of wit and commercial savvy, this rooftop bar overcomes its exposed setting by offering two drinks for the price of one when it rains. Bright young things lounge on leather sofas, pretending not to notice the great city

Muddy Murphy's Irish Pub

views and silently praying for a downpour. ◈ *Map M1 • 331 North Bridge Rd. • 6338-8035 • Open 5pm–1:30am Mon–Fri, 5pm–3am Sat & Sun*

The Balcony Bar

Based in Hereen Arcade, the Balcony Bar's style is billed as Nouveau Morocco, with swings, sofas, storm lanterns, and a rooftop Jacuzzi. DJs play club music and there's a dinner and snack menu. ◈ *Map C5 • 260 Orchard Rd. • 6736-2326 • Open 24 hrs daily*

One Rochester

A gastro-bar in a colonial bungalow, One Rochester's long list of wines and cocktails, as well as a great menu, makes it a hot spot in town. ◈ *Map S3 • No 1 Rochester Park • 6773-0070 • Open 6pm–1am Sun–Fri, 6pm–2am Sat & eve of public holidays, Sun breakfast 9:30am–3pm*

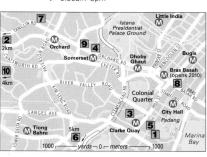

Left **Acid Bar** Centre **Live music at dbl O** Right **Island Bar at Dragonfly**

10 **Nightclubs and Discos**

1 Zouk

Singapore's homegrown Zouk enjoys a worldwide reputation for cutting-edge dance music. This cavernous club is in a converted warehouse with 3 other venues: Phuture, a futuristic club playing experimental music, the loungy Velvet Underground, and the relaxed alfresco Wine Bar. ⊗ *17 Jiak Kim St.* • *6738-2988* • *Open 6pm–3am daily* • *www.zoukclub.com.sg*

2 Zirca

This is the largest of several clubs at The Cannery, a former warehouse in Singapore's party district. Zirca mixes dance music with cabaret and circus shows. Its nightly audio-visual performances feature a huge cast of international and local dancers, aerialists, fire-twirlers, and musicians, plus some of the world's top DJs. ⊗ *Map K2* • *Blk 3 The Cannery #01-02/05–02-01/08, Clarke Quay* • *6235-2292* • *Open 10pm–late Wed–Sat* • *www.the-cannery.com*

3 dbl O

This club holds its ground against the competition as a less pretentious alternative. The main dance floor is supported by smaller venues, such as a down-tempo, alfresco rooftop café, a disco playing earthy R&B and hip-hop, and another playing house grooves. ⊗ *Map J2* • *11 Unity St., #01–24 Robertson Walk* • *6735-2008* • *Open 8pm–3am Tue–Fri, 8pm–4am Sat* • *www.dbl-o.com*

4 Home Club

Supporting the local underground music scene, this dance club regularly features live local indie bands. Music is provided by DJs who spin alternative music, retro, garage, punk, and new wave for a young, arty crowd who lounge on sofas. ⊗ *Map L3* • *20 Upper Circular Rd., B1–01/06, The Riverwalk* • *6538-2928* • *Open 9pm–3am Tue–Thu, 10pm–6am Fri–Sat* • *www.homeclub.com.sg*

5 Insomnia

Named for the 24/7 hours that it keeps, this Hong Kong import features live bands that play pop and rock to a packed dance floor. The CHIJMES *(see p35)* location makes a pretty backdrop for alfresco cocktails and dinners. ⊗ *Map M1* • *CHIJMES #01–21/22/23, 30 Victoria St.* • *6338-6883* • *Open 11am–4am Sun–Tue, 11am–5am Wed–Sat*

Live performances at Insomnia

 Unless otherwise stated, all venues have a cover charge that may vary depending on the night and event.

Acid Bar

A central location makes this venue convenient, drawing in packed crowds for standing-room-only live, Top 40, and pop-rock performances. The dance floor stays rowdy until late. Weekdays are more relaxed with happy-hour drinks. ◎ Map C5 • Peranakan Place, #01-01/02, 180 Orchard Rd. • 6732-6966 • Open 5pm–2am Sun–Thu, 5pm–3am Fri–Sat • No cover charge • www.peranakanplace.com

Velvet Underground lounge at Zouk

Butter Factory

Part dance club, part art gallery, the Butter Factory's walls are decorated with art by local designers and cartoonists, which is for sale. Local trendsetters flock here for hip-hop, R&B, and dance on the swimming pool-style dance floor. ◎ Map J2 • Riverside 48, Robertson Quay #01-03 • 6333-8243 • Open 7–11pm Tue, 8pm–3am Wed & Fri, 7pm–3am Thu, 8pm–4am Sat • www.thebutterfactory.com

Dragonfly

This is Singapore's premier Mandarin nightclub, with live crooners and dance bands playing top hits from the Chinese pop world. The venue has nine clubs offering music to cater for every taste. ◎ Map S3 • St. James Power Station, 3 Sentosa Gateway, #01-01 • 6270-7676 • Open 6pm–6am daily • www.dragonfly.com.sg

Rupee Room

Popular hangout for the local and expatriate Indian population, Rupee Room spins some of India's hottest fusion and dance music, including Bollywood hits and popular northern Indian Bhangra beats. The decor is moody and dramatic, while an attached restaurant serves Indian food. ◎ Map K2 • #01–15 The Foundry, Clarke Quay, 3B River Valley Rd. • 6334-2445 • Open 5pm–2am Sun–Thu, 5pm–6am Fri–Sat • www.harrys.com.sg

Bellini Grande

Enjoy Vegas-style entertainment with an 18-piece pop orchestra featuring international musicians, singers, and dancers at the Bellini Grande. Cuban percussion and singers from Paris are the other global influences. ◎ Map K2 • #01–01 The Foundry, Clarke Quay, 3B River Valley Rd. • 6270-7676 • Open 6pm–3am Sun–Thu, 6pm–4am Fri–Sat • www.bellinigrande.sg

AROUND TOWN

SINGAPORE'S TOP 10

Left **Wak Hai Cheng Bio Temple** Center **A figure at Thian Hock Keng Temple** Right **Ann Siang Hill**

Chinatown

IN 1822, SIR STAMFORD RAFFLES LAID OUT *a town plan that divided Singapore into clearly defined quarters – enclaves that remain distinctive* even today. At the time, the area south of the Singapore River was developing fast with godowns (warehouses) and shipping offices. Behind these, Chinese laborers lived in close quarters. Chinese temples sprang up alongside clan

associations – groups of Chinese who had a common dialect, name, or similar origins, and helped newcomers find work and lodgings. As with Singapore's other enclaves, Chinatown was not homogenous. Indian workers also lived here, especially after the opening of the port at Tanjong Pagar in the mid-1800s. Taoist and Hindu temples, churches and mosques now stand side by side – representing the multicultural spirit that is at the heart of Singapore today.

The lavish Buddha Tooth Relic Temple

🔟 Sights

1. Thian Hock Keng Temple
2. Wak Hai Cheng Bio Temple
3. Sri Mariamman Temple
4. Jamae Chulia Mosque
5. Al-Abrar Mosque
6. Chinatown Heritage Centre
7. Chinatown Pedestrian Mall
8. Singapore City Gallery
9. Buddha Tooth Relic Temple
10. Ann Siang Hill Park

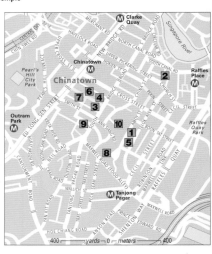

Sri Mariamman Temple façade

Thian Hock Keng Temple

Though a main stop on every tourist itinerary, Thian Hock Keng maintains its authenticity as an important temple for Singapore's Hokkien population. Built in the architectural style of southern Chinese temples, it follows *feng shui*, traditional rules that govern the placement of objects for optimal flow of energy. Though Taoist and dedicated to the goddess Ma Zu (Ma Cho Po), it respects Buddhist teachings, too, with a shrine of Bodhisattva Guanyin and a swastika symbol embellishing its outer walls *(see pp12–13)*.

Wak Hai Cheng Bio Temple

A Taoist center for the Teochew community, this small temple seems almost magical. Inside the courtyard, rows of smoking spiral joss sticks are suspended from a grid, while the temple itself, with its sloping roof covered with figurines of colorful ceramic shards, is

Jamae Chulia Mosque

curiously juxtaposed against the glass and steel skyscrapers that completely surround it. Two halls are dedicated to Ma Zu and Xuan Tian Shang Di, a powerful god who is believed to control the elements. ✆ *Map L4 • 30-B Phillip St. • Open 9am–6pm daily*

Sri Mariamman Temple

Sri Mariamman, or "Mother Goddess" as she is known to Hindus, is honored at this temple, Singapore's oldest Hindu place of worship. It was established in 1823 by Narayana Pillay, a government clerk who arrived aboard Raffles' ship and decided to stay. The current temple was built in 1843 by former Indian convicts. Sri Mariamman is believed to cure diseases, so it is appropriate that free medical services are available here.
✆ *Map K4 • 244 South Bridge Rd.*
• 6223-4064 • Open 8am–8pm daily
• www.heb.gov.sg

Jamae Chulia Mosque

The Chulias were Muslims engaged in trade and money changing who came from India's southern coast. They financed the building of the nearby Al-Abrar Mosque as well as this one. The impressive façade of Jamae Chulia is southern Indian in style, with latticework embellishment and two tall minarets with *mihrab* (small niches) carved in the sides. Cloaks are available inside the entrance to cover visitors wearing shorts or sleeveless tops. ✆ *Map K4 • 18 South Bridge Rd. • 6221-4165 • Open 9am–6pm daily, closed noon–3pm Fri*

 For more Singapore places of worship, **See pp38-9**

Shoppers at Chinatown Pedestrian Mall

5 Al-Abrar Mosque

Once the island's most important mosque, Al-Abrar was originally a seaside hut built from wood and *attap* (thatch), that served the community living and working in the area – hence its name "Koochoo Palli," or hut mosque. Squeezed between shophouses, its façade blends in with the city. It is very quiet, serving a handful of workers in the area, while most Muslims prefer to pray at mosques closer to home. ◈ *Map L5 • 192 Telok Ayer St. • 6220-6306 • Open 11:30am–9pm Sat–Thu, 10am–9pm Fri*

6 Chinatown Heritage Centre

This museum, located in three restored shophouses in the heart of Chinatown, illustrates the harsh conditions in which the Chinese community lived and worked in Singapore's early days.

Doctor's room, Chinatown Heritage Centre

Occupying three levels, it re-creates scenes from old shops, coffee-shops, and living cubicles, with an interesting exhibit dedicated to the "four evils" of gambling, opium smoking, prostitution, and secret societies. ◈ *Map K4 • 48 Pagoda St. • 6325-2878 • Open 9am–8pm daily • www.chinatownheritage.com.sg • Adm*

7 Chinatown Pedestrian Mall

Closed to vehicles, these two streets lined with stalls sell a jumble of gifts, trinkets, and treasures, mostly from China. There are also batiks and carved wood items, most likely from Indonesia, and lacquerware and silk items from Vietnam. Behind the stalls, stores sell pricier gifts, art, and antiques. Nearby Smith Street is closed to traffic in the evenings as tables are set and food is served from roadside stalls. ◈ *Map K4 • Trengganu St. & Pagoda St. • Open 10am–11pm daily*

8 Singapore City Gallery

The Urban Redevelopment Authority oversees the use of the island's scarce land resource. For this gallery, the agency has built an amazing model of the city's central area, providing a fantastic overview of its heritage

 Shophouses are row houses with a shop at the front, which were introduced to Singapore by Chinese immigrants.

hotspots and an insight into urban planning. A 45-minute tour is conducted on weekdays starting at 11:30am. ✈ Map K5
• 45 Maxwell Rd. • 6321-8321
• Open 9am–5pm Mon–Sat
• www.ura.gov.sg

Buddha Tooth Relic Temple
This complex, completed in 2007 at a cost of S$53 million, houses a sacred tooth relic of the Buddha. The building contains halls for prayer and meditation, a theater, museums, an exhibition center, a gift shop, and a teahouse. While the layout is based on the Buddhist order of the cosmos, the architecture is inspired by the Tang Dynasty of China. Shorts, skirts, and sleeveless tops are not allowed. ✈ Map K4 • 288 South Bridge Rd. • 6220-0220 • Open 7am–7pm daily • www.btrts.org.sg

Ann Siang Hill Park
Chinatown and Tanjong Pagar were once covered in hills, but most have been levelled. Ann Siang Hill is one of the few that remains. This park stretches along the hilltop, with stairs and boardwalks offering views over shophouse rooftops. ✈ Map K4, L4 • Park entrances: Amoy St. & Club St.

Model of the city at Singapore City Gallery

A Day in Chinatown

Morning

🕐 From the Chinatown MRT, take the overhead walkway across Eu Tong Sen Street and New Bridge Road to Pagoda Street. Start with the **Chinatown Heritage Centre** on Pagoda Street which will give you an overview of the neighborhood's heritage. Outside, meander through the stalls of the **Chinatown Pedestrian Mall** at Pagoda and Trengganu streets, where shops sell drinks and snacks. Nearby on South Bridge Road is the perfect example of multicultural harmony in Singapore. Here, you can visit the **Jamae Chulia Mosque** (see p67) on the corner of Mosque Street, the **Sri Mariamman Temple** on Temple Street, and the **Buddha Tooth Relic Temple** on Sago Street.

Afternoon

Have an authentic local lunch and something cool to drink at one of the food-stalls at the **Maxwell Food Centre** (see p56) opposite the **Buddha Tooth Relic Temple**. If you prefer to eat lunch in a restaurant, stroll up Ann Siang Hill to Club Street where you will find a selection of chic Asian and international restaurants in restored shophouses. After lunch, take a stroll along Club Street to admire the architecture, then take the shortcut through **Ann Siang Hill Park** to Amoy Street where many legal, public relations, and advertising firms have offices. The park ends just behind the **Thian Hock Keng Temple** (see pp12–13).

Left **Reflexology at the Fuji Centre** Center **Calligraphy** Right **Chinese Checkers**

🔟 Chinese Cultural Experiences

1 Eu Yan Sang Clinic for Traditional Medicine
Over 45 percent of Singaporeans use traditional Chinese medicine. The Eu Yan Sang dispensary has 20 branches in Singapore and Malaysia. *Map K4 • 273 South Bridge Rd. • 6223-5085 • Open 8:30am–6pm Mon–Sat • www.euyansang.com*

2 Eu Yan Sang Clinic for Acupuncture
Eu Yan Sang Clinic also offers acupuncture – thin steel needles stimulate positive energy in the body to treat illness and disease. *Map K4 • 273 South Bridge Rd. • 6223-5085 • Open 9am–6pm Mon–Sat • Adm*

3 The Tea Chapter
Learn the art of the traditional Chinese tea ceremony while you relax in this quaint café. *Map K5 • 9A 11 Neil Rd. • 6226-1175 • Open 11am–11pm daily • www.tea-chapter.com.sg • Adm*

4 Chinese Theatre Circle
Traditional Chinese opera is preserved with costume, music, and demonstrations of theatrical technique. *Map K4 • 5 Smith St. • 6323-4862 • Open 7–9pm Fri–Sat • www.ctcopera.com.sg • Adm*

5 Fuji Reflexology Centre
At this clinic, reflexology techniques soothe tired feet through application of firm pressure to various zones on the foot that correspond to parts of the body. *Map K4 • 9A Trengganu St. • 6223-7363 • Open 11am–9pm daily • Adm*

6 Wet Market
The floors of this market are hosed with water daily. It sells fruit, vegetables, meats, and dried goods. *Map K4 • Chinatown Complex • Open 5am–noon Tue–Sun*

7 Siong Moh Trading
This store sells fake banknotes and paper replicas of luxury goods ("hell money"), burned to reach departed souls in the afterlife. *Map K4 • 39 Mosque St. • 6224-3125 • Open 9am–5pm Mon–Sat*

8 Chinatown Night Market
A chance to watch sidewalk calligraphers translate foreign names into Chinese characters (see p72). *Map K4 • Pagoda St.*

9 Da Wei Arts n Crafts
This store stocks Chinese art supplies such as rice paper, ink, brushes, and stones to mix ink. *Map K4 • 270 South Bridge Rd. • 6224-5058 • Open 10:30am–7:30pm daily*

10 Chinese Checkers
Amid touristy shops, old locals still gather to play checkers. *Map K4 • Sago St. & Trengganu St.*

Price Categories

For a three-course meal for one with a non-alchoholic drink (or equivalent meal), taxes, and extra charges.

$	under S$20
$$	S$20–30
$$$	S$30–50
$$$$	S$50–70
$$$$$	over S$70

Left IndoChine at Club Street

Restaurants

1 Hometown Restaurant

This eatery serves dishes from China's Sichuan province. The cuisine generously uses dried chili, black pepper, and salt. ◉ *Map K4 • 9 Smith St. • 6372-1602 • Open 11am–3pm & 5–10pm daily • $$*

2 Yum Cha

An old-style shophouse serving delicious dim sum, Cantonese treats, and crispy pastries. ◉*Map K4 • 20 Trengganu St. • 6372-1717 • Open 11am–11pm Mon–Fri, 9am–11pm Sat–Sun • $$*

3 IndoChine

Silk, incense, and candles create a lounge ambience in which to enjoy food from Laos, Vietnam, and Cambodia. ◉ *Map K4 • 49B Club St. • 6323-0503 • Open noon–2:30pm & 6:30–10:30pm Mon–Sat • $$$$*

4 Da Paolo il Ristorante

The elegant Da Paolo has Italian specialties such as rack of lamb and spaghetti with squid ink. ◉ *Map K4 • 80 Club St. • 6224-7081 • Open 11:30am–2:30pm & 6:30–10:30pm daily • $$$$*

5 Grand Shanghai

Here, Shanghainese seafood is lightly cooked and served in a 1920s ambience. ◉ *390 Havelock Rd. • 6836-6866 • Open noon–2:30pm & 6:30–11pm Tue–Fri & Sun, 6:30–11pm Sat • $$$$*

6 The Universal Restaurant and Wine Bar

This offers contemporary Australian cuisine complemented by a wine list that boasts 300 labels. The ambience is cozy and mod in equal parts. ◉ *Map K5 • 36 Duxton Rd. • 6325-0188 • Open noon–2pm & 6:30–10pm Mon–Fri, 6:30–10pm Sat • $$$$$*

7 Blue Ginger

This is the place to try Peranakan cuisine, such as *ayam buah keluak* – chicken curry with Indonesian nuts. ◉ *Map K5 • 97 Tanjong Pagar Rd. • 6222-3928 • Open noon–2:30pm & 6:30–10:30pm daily • $$*

8 Annalakshmi

Enjoy Indian vegetarian fare at this place operated by the Temple of Fine Arts, a charity for art and music. ◉ *Map K4 • #B1–02 133 New Bridge Rd. • 6339-9993 • Open 11:30am–3pm & 6:30–9:30pm Tue–Sun, 6:30–9:30pm Mon • No set price*

9 Taj Authentic Indian Cuisine

Home of what may be the best chicken and mutton *biryani* in Singapore. ◉ *Map K4 • 214 South Bridge Rd. • 6226-6020 • Open 11:30am–8:30pm daily• $*

10 Ci Yan Organic Health Food

Enjoy Chinese vegetarian meals from a menu that changes daily. ◉ *Map K4 • 8 Smith St. • 6225-9026 • Open noon–10:30pm daily • $*

Note: Unless otherwise stated, all restaurants accept credit cards and serve vegetarian meals.

Left **Joe Arts & Crafts Gallery** Center **Souvenir display on Pagoda Street** Right **Antique Pavilion**

Shopping

1 Yue Hwa Chinese Emporium
This emporium is recommended for the variety of Chinese handicrafts it stocks, right from silk clothing to hand-embroidered linen, jade jewelry, and gifts at affordable prices. ✆ *Map K4 • 70 Eu Tong Sen St. • 6538-4222 • Open 11am–9pm Sun–Fri, 11am–10pm Sat*

2 Tiandu Art Gallery
Chinese calligraphy and brush paintings imported from China are on sale here. ✆ *Map K4 • #03–07 Chinatown Point • 6538-8546 • Open noon–6pm daily*

3 Joe Arts & Crafts Gallery
Every shelf here is packed with figurines and collectibles. ✆ *Map K4 • #03–79 Chinatown Point • 6534-1728 • Open 2–8pm daily*

4 World Arts & Crafts
With a collection from as far as China and South America, this store sells crystals set in jewelry or in natural rock forms. ✆ *Map K4 • #03–78 Chinatown Point • 6532-0056 • Open noon–7pm daily*

5 Gtar Cultural & Arts Centre
Gtar sells Chinese musical instruments, such as the *liuqin* (a lute) and the *erhu* (a flute). ✆ *Map K4 • #03–64 Chinatown Point • 6536-6383 • Open noon–8pm Fri–Wed*

6 Chinatown Seal Carving
Craftsmen here will translate your name or message into Chinese characters and carve them onto your choice of stone "chops" (Chinese stamps). ✆ *Map K4 • #03–77 Chinatown Point • 6534-1128 • Open 11am–8pm daily*

7 Antique Pavilion
Singapore's largest Chinese fabric wholesaler, this store sells placemats, pillow covers, and duvets, plus pashminas and silk shawls. ✆ *Map K4 • 56 Pagoda St. • 6327-1671 • Open 10am–8:30pm daily*

8 Chinatown Night Market
The name is misleading, since stalls open during the day, too. They sell every kind of souvenir, but shop around to compare prices. ✆ *Map K4 • Pagoda St. & Trengganu St. • Open 11am–11pm daily*

9 Chinatown Complex
This complex sells mostly household goods, but there are some unusual finds for the bargain hunter. ✆ *Map K4 • Sago St. & Trengganu St. • Opening times vary*

10 Lukisan Art Gallery
Dealing in contemporary Asian art, Lukisan sells works from China, Vietnam, and Indonesia. ✆ *Map K4 • 26 Smith St. • 6410-9663 • Open 2–9pm Tue–Sun*

Left **Egg tarts at Tong Heng confectionery** Right **Red Dot Design Museum**

TOP 10 Best of the Rest

1 Yue Hwa
Traditional Chinese dresses called *cheongsam* can be bought in most markets. There is a good selection available at this store. Ⓢ *Map K4 • 70 Eu Tong Sen St.* • *6538-4222 • Open 11am–9pm Sun–Fri, 11am–10pm Sat*

2 Bee Cheng Hiang
Specializing in *bak kwa* – slices of barbecued pork – in many flavors, Bee Cheng Hiang often has lines going around the block. Ⓢ *Map K4 • 189 New Bridge Rd.* • *6223-7059 • Open 8am–9pm daily*

3 Speakers' Corner
This stage in a public park is the official platform for public speaking in Singapore. Speakers must not issue racial or religious slurs. Ⓢ *Map K3 • Hong Lim Park, Upper Pickering St. & New Bridge Rd.* • *Open 7am–7pm daily*

4 Fuk Tak Chi Museum
Once a small shrine serving the Cantonese and Hakka dialect groups, Fuk Tak displays a series of artifacts collected from the local Chinese community. Ⓢ *Map L4 • 76 Telok Ayer St. • 6532-7868* • *Open 10am–10pm daily*

5 Xin Jing Jing Restaurant
This café specializes in Chinese and local desserts, such as the house specialty,

mango and coconut ice, and mango with pomelo sago. Ⓢ *Map K4 • 24 Smith St. • 6221-5531* • *Open noon–11pm daily*

6 Tai Chong Kok
Traditionally filled with lotus seed paste, the modern mooncakes here come in many flavors. Ⓢ *Map K4 • 34 Sago St.* • *Open 11am–2pm Mon–Sat*

7 Tong Heng Confectionery
This patisserie serves Chinese-style egg tarts, a local version of the Portuguese recipe. Ⓢ *Map K4 • 285 South Bridge Rd.* • *6223-0398 • Open 9am–10pm daily*

8 Red Dot Design Museum
See works by winners of the international Red Dot Design Award, one of the world's most renowned design competitions. Ⓢ *Map K5 • 28 Maxwell Rd. • 6534-7194* • *Open 11am–6pm Mon, Tue & Fri; 11am–8pm Sat–Sun, closed Wed & Thu • Adm*

9 Club Street
Once home to Chinese clan associations, this street has boutiques and restaurants. Ⓢ *Map K4, L4*

10 Chinese Weekly Entertainment Club
Built in 1892, this mansion was once a draw for socialites. Ⓢ *Map K4 • 76 Club St. • No public access*

Left **Serangoon Road** Center **Exhibit at the Malay Heritage Centre** Right **Mustafa Centre**

Little India and Kampong Glam

I N SINGAPORE'S EARLY DAYS, *ranchers settled and raised cattle in the area that is now Little India. The industry blossomed, supported by Indian labor. The government later opened brick kilns and lime pits that also relied on Indian workers. Thus, Little India was not a planned ethnic quarter but sprang from the community that gravitated here. Today, stores selling goods*

Inside Sri Srinivasa Perumal Temple

from India lend it authenticity. Kampong Glam was allocated to the Sultan of Singapore in Raffles' 1822 town plan. It attracted other Muslim residents such as Malays, Bugis (from Sulawesi), and Arabs. Bugis immigrants set up ship-building firms, while some Arab companies are still in business today. A recent resurgence of Arabic culture can be seen here in the cafés and sheesha lounges, and in some stores.

Sights

1. Serangoon Road
2. Sri Veeramakaliamman Temple
3. Sri Srinivasa Perumal Temple
4. Sakya Muni Buddha Gaya Temple
5. Abdul Gafoor Mosque
6. Mustafa Centre
7. Arab Street
8. Sultan Mosque
9. Hajjah Fatimah Mosque
10. Malay Heritage Centre

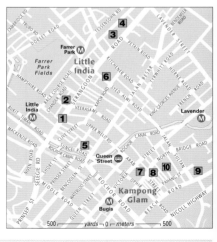

Serangoon Road

This avenue is the heart of Little India, an enclave that has escaped modernization amid a changing Singapore. Family-run stores still operate from old shophouses with peeling paint, covered walkways, and a jumble of goods. A number of Indians settled in Singapore still come here to buy items from India, from clothing to groceries and cere-monial treasures. Inside some of the stores, traders, such as spice grinders, laundrymen, and goldsmiths, operate as they have done for decades. ◈ Map F4, H4

Ganesh statue at the Sri Veeramakaliamman Temple

Sri Veeramakaliamman Temple

Since its humble beginnings in the mid-19th century, this temple has been associated with the laboring classes, as it was built mainly by and for workers in the area. It was constructed for the worship of Kali, a divine mother figure who provides comfort to worshippers far from home. As with all Hindu temples in Singapore, the colorful figures on the roof were created by skilled craftsmen brought in from southern India especially for the job (see pp16–17).

Sri Srinivasa Perumal Temple

The first temple in Singapore to be built for the worship of Vishnu, Sri Srinivasa Perumal temple has an impressive gopuram with more than five tiers of figurines, including representations of Vishnu's various incarnations as well as his steed, the half-man-half-eagle Garuda. Part of the Hindu trinity, Vishnu is associated with protection, while Brahma is associated with creation, and Shiva with destruction. This temple is also the starting point for the Thaipusam and Thimithi festivals (see pp44–5).
◈ Map G2 • 397 Serangoon Rd. • 6298-5771 • Open 6:30am–noon and 6–9pm daily • www.heb.gov.sg/sspt

Sakya Muni Buddha Gaya Temple

This small Buddhist temple is also known as the Temple of a Thousand Lights, thanks to the 989 lights surrounding the main Buddha image, turned on for special ceremonies. Around the base of the main altar, painted murals depict episodes from the life of the Buddha. Behind the altar, a small doorway leads to an inner chamber with an image of the reclining Buddha. The temple has many Thai aesthetic influences handed down from its founder, who was a Thai monk. ◈ Map G2 • 366 Race Course Rd. • 6294-0714 • Open 8am–4:45pm daily

Sakya Muni Buddha Gaya Temple

For more Singapore places of worship See pp38–9

75

Istana Kampong Glam

In 1824, Sultan Hussein signed away his sovereign rights over Singapore to the East India Company in return for a plot of land and an annual stipend. After his death, his son Sultan Ali built Istana Kampong Glam on the land. Royal fortunes dwindled and in 1897 a court ruled that the estate belonged to the crown. The royal family was later resettled and the state turned the palace into the Malay Heritage Centre.

5 Abdul Gafoor Mosque

This mosque is a mix of Islamic and European architecture, with stately columns supporting Moorish arches. A sun motif above the main entrance contains names of the 25 prophets of Islam in delicate calligraphy in each of its rays. This mosque compound includes the shophouses around it. The rent from these has contributed to its restoration. ◈ Map F4, G4 • 41 Dunlop Street • 6295-4209 • Open 9:30am–9pm (except prayer times 12:30–1:30pm, 4:45–5:30pm) daily

6 Mustafa Centre

This enormous department store snakes through two city blocks which offer 24-hour shopping for a huge range of Indian products. There is everything from ordinary store goods, offered at excellent discounts, to a stunning collection of intricately designed traditional treasures in the gold department. The store also has a large collection of saris, costume jewelry, instant curry mixes, and textiles. ◈ Map G3 • 145 Syed Alwi Rd. • 6295-5855 • www.mustafa.com.sg

7 Arab Street

Named for the Arab traders who were among the earliest foreign settlers, Arab Street is the main thoroughfare in Kampong Glam, Singapore's Muslim quarter. The original stores here traded in spices and textiles, while today browsers can find batiks, baskets, fabrics, and items from Indonesia and the Middle East. ◈ Map G4, G5, H5

8 Sultan Mosque

The most important mosque in Singapore, Sultan Mosque was built using contributions from the Muslim community. Even glass bottles donated from the poor were used for the band at the base of the onion dome. The mosque's governing body is made up of two members from each ethnic

Abdul Gafoor Mosque

Shophouses are row houses with a shop at the front, which were introduced to Singapore by Chinese immigrants.

Prayer hall at the Sultan Mosque

group of the local Muslim community – Malays, Javanese, Bugis, Arabs, Tamils, and North Indians *(see pp14–15)*.

9 Hajjah Fatimah Mosque
A local businesswoman, Hajjah Fatimah lived at this site in a house that was repeatedly burglarized and eventually set on fire. In gratitude for her escape, she decided to build a mosque here. Built in around 1846, the building is a mix of European, Chinese, and Malay architecture. Most interesting is the tilting minaret, Singapore's take on Italy's Leaning Tower of Pisa.
🕉 *Map H5 • 4001 Beach Rd. • 6297-2774 • Open 10am–noon, 2:30–9pm daily*

10 Malay Heritage Centre
Originally Istana Kampong Glam, the official residence of the Sultan of Singapore, this building is an example of the Neoclassical architecture popular in the early 1800s. It is believed to have been designed by G.D. Coleman, the architect behind many of Singapore's civic buildings and churches. In 2006 it was restored and reopened as the Malay Heritage Centre.
🕉 *Map H4 • 85 Sultan Gate • 6391-0450 • Compound: 8am–9pm daily; Museum: 10am–6pm Tue–Sun, 1–6pm Mon • Adm (museum) • www.malayheritage.org.sg*

Exploring Little India and Kampong Glam

Morning

🕐 From the Little India MRT station, walk one block to the start of Serangoon Road at the corner of Bukit Timah Road. Here, **Little India Arcade** *(see p82)* hosts a nice collection of stores that sell imported goods from India. Follow Serangoon Road to **Sri Veeramakaliamman Temple** *(see pp16–17)* to witness the vibrant traditions of a Hindu temple. Farther down Serangoon Road is **Sri Srinivasa Perumal Temple** *(see pp74–5)*, which, with fewer crowds than Sri Veeramakaliamman Temple, is a more peaceful environment in which to contemplate Hinduism. Next, take Perumal Road beside the temple to Race Course Road. Turn right and walk to the **Sakya Muni Buddha Gaya Temple** *(see pp74–5)* which is on the right.

Afternoon

From Little India take a short taxi ride to **Kampong Glam** and try a relaxing Egyptian-style lunch at **Altazzag** *(see p83)* or authentic spicy local fare at **Sabar Menanti Restaurant** *(see p83)*. In Kampong Glam, start at the **Sultan Mosque** *(see pp14–15)* for a glimpse inside the religious heart of the neighborhood. From the mosque stroll down **Bussorah Mall** *(see p81)* and browse through batiks, antiques, and other souvenirs from the region. At Baghdad Street turn left and walk to Sultan Gate. Turn left and continue to the **Malay Heritage Centre** for an introduction to Malay culture and history.

Left **ANSA Picture Framing and Art Gallery** Right **Garlands of roses, marigolds, and jasmine**

Top 10 Little India Experiences

1 Century 10 Ayurvedic Therapy
Traditional Indian medicine is said to have been practiced for more than 5,000 years. Treatments may involve herbal medicines, baths, diet, and massage. ⊗ *Map F4 • 27 Campbell Lane • 6341-7097 • Open 9am–8pm Tue–Sun, 11am–4pm Mon*

2 Selvi's
Henna artists apply a non-toxic paste to the hands in intricate patterns, leaving behind a tattooed effect. ⊗ *Map F4 • Serangoon Rd. & Little India Arcade • 9144-5284 • Open 9am–8pm Mon–Sat, 8am–4pm alternate Sun*

3 Sajeev Studio
This photographer dresses men and women in traditional Indian clothing, jewelry, and make-up for keepsake portraits. ⊗ *Map F4 • 23 Kerbau Rd. • 6296-6537 • Open 10am–10pm daily*

4 Serangoon Ladies Centre
There is a selection of ready-made *cholis*, or blouses, and petticoats worn under saris here. ⊗ *Map F4 • 3 Kerbau Rd. • 6297-4650 • Open 11:30am–8:30pm Mon–Sat*

5 The Yoga Shop
This yoga center offers books and other yoga-related materials, and can also direct you to free classes. ⊗ *Map F3 • 10 Kerbau Rd. • 6467-1742 • Open noon–8:30pm Mon–Fri, 10:30am–8:30pm Sat, 10:30am–6pm Sun*

6 ANSA Picture Framing and Art Gallery
Browse through colorful portraits of Hindu deities along with some secular works. ⊗ *Map F3 • 29 Kerbau Rd. • 6295-6605 • Open 9:30am–9:30pm Mon–Sat, 10:30am–3:30pm Sun*

7 Spice Grinding
In this shophouse, Indian spices are ground in electric mills that spew scented powder. ⊗ *Map F4 • 2 Cuff Rd. • Open 9:30am–6:30pm Tue–Sun*

8 Flower Garlands
Garlands of fresh flowers are sewn together by hand and sold on street corners in this area. ⊗ *Map F4 • Campbell Lane & Buffalo Rd*

9 Betel Nuts
The *areca* seed palm is wrapped by street sellers in a peppery leaf, to be chewed. ⊗ *Map F4 • Campbell Lane & Buffalo Rd*

10 Fortune Teller
An old man's parakeet will tell your fortune with cards. He keeps no regular hours or location. ⊗ *Map F4 • Serangoon Rd*

Left *Baju Kurong* at **Mona J. Boutique** Right **Bussorah Mall**

🔟 Kampong Glam Experiences

Mona J. Boutique
1 This store sells *baju kurong*, or "clothes that cover." They express the Malay ladies' flair for color and style. ◈ *Map H5 • 41 Bussorah St. • 6297-1498 • Open 10:30am–6:30pm Mon–Sat*

Pyramid Dancer
2 This dazzling array of Middle Eastern artifacts and bejeweled costumes for bellydancers is testament to the continuing Arab influence in these parts. ◈ *Map H5 • 38 Arab St. • 6396-7598 • Open 10am–7pm daily • www.pyramiddancer.com.sg*

Sarabat Stall
3 This sells a thick mixture of sweetened condensed milk and tea, poured between two cups to make it frothy. ◈ *Map H5 • 21 Baghdad St. • Open 6:30am–11:30pm daily*

Wayan Retreat Balinese Spa
4 Wayan uses baths, wraps, scrubs, and facials to rejuvenate and relax. ◈ *Map H5 • 61 Bussorah St. • 6392-0035 • Open 10am–9pm Mon–Fri, 10am–8pm Sat, 10am–6pm Sun (closed public holidays)*

Straits Records
5 For the best selection of local indie recordings, plus information about gigs. ◈ *Map G5 • 22 Bali Lane • Open 3pm until late daily*

Café Le Claire
6 A popular late-night hangout for fans of *sheesha*, the traditional Arab water pipe, this café serves Middle Eastern cuisine. ◈ *Map H5 • 39 Arab St. • 6292-0979 • Open 10–3:30am Mon–Thu, 10–5:30am Fri–Sat*

Haji Lane
7 A narrow back alley with offbeat stores that sell locally designed clothing and imported oddities. ◈ *Map G5, H5 • 15 minutes walk from Bugis MRT*

Bussorah Mall
8 A wide, palm-fringed avenue full of unique stores selling everything from souvenirs to interesting antiques and craft items. ◈ *Map H5 • Bussorah St.*

Muslim Cemetery
9 The gravestones here look haphazard, but square stones mark men's graves and round ones those of women. ◈ *Map H4 • Corner of Victoria St. & Jalan Kubor*

Golden Mile Complex
10 Singapore's Little Thailand attracts residents with groceries, traditional goods, and authentic Thai food. ◈ *Map H5 • 5001 Beach Rd. • Open 10am–10pm daily*

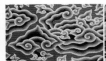

Left **Hand-dyed batik at Basharahil Brothers** Center **Mustafa Centre** Right **Rishi Handicrafts**

🔟 Shopping

1 Mustafa Centre
Though 24-hour Mustafa Centre sells everything under the sun, its best buys are Indian imports – silk saris, gold jewelry, and woven textiles *(see p76)*.

2 Little India Arcade
A cluster of stores here sells costume jewelry, tapestries, Bollywood DVDs, incense, leather goods, and Indian fashions. ◎ *Map F4 • 48 Serangoon Rd. • 6295-5998 • Open 10am–10pm daily*

3 Tekka Market
This temporary set-up offers a wet market and hawker stalls as well as stores stocking inexpensive Indian clothing. ◎ *Map F3 • Race Course Rd. • Open 6am–10pm daily*

4 StyleMart
A boutique specializing in fine, formal Indian fashions, such as embroidered and beaded silks and brocades. ◎ *Map F4 • 149–151 Selegie Rd. • 6338-2073 • Open 11am–8:45pm Mon–Sat, noon–6:45pm Sun*

5 Handlooms
Handcrafted silk and cotton textiles, pillow covers, bedspreads, tablecloths, and clothing are reasonably priced here. ◎ *Map F4 • Little India Arcade, 48 Serangoon Rd. • 6293-2861 • Open 10am–7:30pm Mon–Sat, 10am–5pm Sun*

6 Melor's Curios
Along with a collection of antiques and collectibles from Indonesia, Melor's sells carved wood furniture and objets d'art. ◎ *Map H5 • 39 Bussorah St. • 6292-3934 • Open 10am–6pm daily*

7 Jamal Kazura Aromatics
This store sells oil-based fragrances for Muslim women who wish to avoid contact with alcohol. ◎ *Map H5 • 21 Bussorah St. • 6293-3320 • Open 9:30am–6:30pm daily*

8 Basharahil Brothers
Cotton and silk batik cloth, imported from Indonesia, is sold here by the meter or in the form of sarongs, placemats, tablecloths, and napkins. ◎ *Map H5 • 101 Arab St. • 6296-0432 • Open 10am–6pm Mon–Sat, 11am–5pm Sun*

9 Rishi Handicrafts
All sorts of baskets, woven hats, mats, and bags, mostly from Indonesia and China, are available at this Arab Street landmark. ◎ *Map H5 • 1 Bussorah St. • 6298-2408 • Open 10am–6pm daily*

🔟 Kupu Kupu
A boutique that has clothing inspired by Southeast Asian silhouettes and fashioned from embellished batik. ◎ *Map H5 • 32 Bussorah St. • 6294-2180 • Open 10am–6pm Mon–Sat, 10am–5pm Sun*

Price Categories

For a three-course meal for one with a non-alchoholic drink (or equivalent meal), taxes, and extra charges.

$	under S$20
$$	S$20–30
$$$	S$30–50
$$$$	S$50–70
$$$$$	over S$70

Left **Tepak Sireh Restoran** Right **Muthu's Curry**

🔟 Restaurants

1 Jaggi's Northern Indian Cuisine
Enjoy delicious Indian curries, plus meats and breads from Jaggi's tandoor oven. 🄫 Map F3 • 34/36 Race Course Rd. • 6296-6141 • Open 11:30am–3:15pm, 6:30–10:30pm Mon–Sat, 10:30am–3:30pm Sun (closed last Sun each month) • $

2 Komala Villas
One of the quickest lunches around. The specialty, *dosai*, is a hot pancake served with gravy. 🄫 Map F4 • 76 Serangoon Rd. • 6294-3294 • Open 7am–10:30pm daily • $

3 Muthu's Curry
Home of Singapore's favorite fish-head curry, Muthu's serves southern Indian dishes, too. 🄫 Map F3 • 138 Race Course Rd. • 6392-1722 • Open 10:30am–10:30pm daily • $$

4 The Banana Leaf Apollo
Along Singapore's famed "curry row," this place is named for the leaf on which southern Indian cuisine is traditionally served. It also offers northern Indian dishes. 🄫 Map F3 • 56/58 Race Course Rd. • 6297-1595 • Open 10:30am–10:30pm daily • $$

5 The French Stall
This French bistro in a Singaporean shophouse is a lively, popular spot. 🄫 Map G2 • 544 Serangoon Rd. • 6299-3544 • Open 3–10pm Tue–Sun • $$

6 Sabar Menanti Restaurant
Here you can try halal meats, seafood, and vegetables stewed in spices. The Sumatran rice dish *nasi padang* is worth the waiting in line. 🄫 Map H5 • 48 & 50 Kandahar St. • 6396-6919 • Open 8:30am–6pm daily • $

7 Nabin's Experience Arabia
Though mostly Arabic, Nabin's serves other cuisines, too. Belly dancers perform occasionally. 🄫 Map G5 • 27 Bali Lane • 6398-0530 • Open 10am–11pm Mon–Fri, 10am–5am Sat–Sun • $$

8 Tepak Sireh Restoran
Once part of the royal compound, this is now a restaurant serving dishes such as *nasi padang*. 🄫 Map H5 • 73 Sultan Gate • 6393-4373 • Open 11:30am–2:30pm and 6:30–9:30pm Mon–Sat • $$

9 Altazzag Egyptian Restaurant
Kebabs, salads, specialty teas, and *sheesha* make this a popular night hangout. 🄫 Map H5 • 24 Haji Lane • 6295-5024 • Open noon–3am Mon–Sat, 5pm–3am Sun • $$

10 Zam Zam
Zam Zam is famed for *murtabak*, an Indian bread filled with onion, meat, and egg, dipped in curry. 🄫 Map G5 • 697/699 North Bridge Rd. • 6298-7011 • Open 8am–11pm daily • $

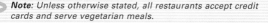

Note: Unless otherwise stated, all restaurants accept credit cards and serve vegetarian meals.

Left **The History Gallery at the National Museum of Singapore** Right **Singapore Art Museum**

Colonial District

BEFORE THE ARRIVAL OF SIR THOMAS STAMFORD RAFFLES, *Singapore was a small fishing village surrounded by jungle. In time, the jungle gave way to building programs to house the local, and eventually colonial, government. The hill overlooking the district was cleared and a governor's residence built on top, with botanical gardens. In the 1800s, the district expanded. Many existing buildings date from this era. The oldest place in the city is Fort Canning, a hilltop park. Here a grave is tended, believed to be that of Iskandar Shah, who settled in Singapore before Raffles but moved on to found Melaka in Malaysia.*

🔟 Sights

1. Fort Canning Park
2. Old Parliament House
3. Victoria Theatre and Concert Hall
4. The Empress Building/ Asian Civilisations Museum
5. Statue of Raffles
6. Raffles Hotel
7. City Hall and the Supreme Court
8. National Museum of Singapore
9. Singapore Art Museum
10. Singapore Philatelic Museum

Statue of Raffles

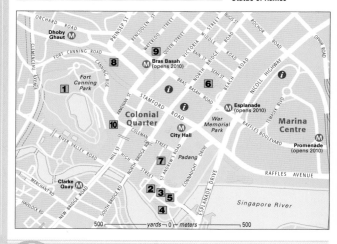

Fort Canning Park

Raffles built his home at this site, but it was replaced by Fort Canning in 1860. The military stronghold atop the park's hill was impressive, but it proved useless protection as its cannons could not reach as far as the harbor. The fort was demolished in 1929, but a Gothic gate remains. Military offices now house art groups and the lawns host concerts. The underground bunkers, known as the Battle Box, are now a World War II exhibit *(see pp40–41)*. ◎ *Map K1–2, L1–2 • 51 Canning Rise • 6332-1302 • Open 24 hours daily • www.nparks.gov.sg*

A wartime meeting re-created in Fort Canning Park

Old Parliament House

Before Raffles' Town Plan could be executed *(see p86)*, construction began on the first modern structure in Singapore. It was built as a private mansion for a Scottish merchant, but because Raffles had intended the area for civic use, Maxwell's House was later sold to the government. In 1999, having outgrown the space, the government left the building for the new granite Parliament House next to it *(see pp10–11)*.

Victoria Theatre and Concert Hall

The Town Hall, completed in 1862, was the first structure purpose-built for the colonial government. It was designed on what was then a grand scale, but the government soon outgrew the premises. In 1909 it was converted into a theater. The adjacent concert hall, now home to the Singapore Symphony Orchestra, was finished in 1905. Both venues were then dedicated to Queen Victoria. ◎ *Map M3 • 9 Empress Place • 6339-6120 • Open only to concert ticket holders*

The Empress Building/ Asian Civilisations Museum

Since Maxwell's House was ill-suited to the growing colonial administration, a new government office was built. The oldest part was erected in 1864, with three extensions being added before it was reopened in 1905 as the Empress Place Building. It continued to be used for offices until the 1980s. Among these was the Registry of Births and Deaths – it was said that every Singaporean passed through its doors. In 2002, the building became the Asian Civilisations Museum *(see pp10–11)*.

Victoria Theatre and Concert Hall

The courtyard at Raffles Hotel

Raffles' Town Plan of 1822

In 1822 Sir Stamford Raffles formed a committee to design a plan to divide Singapore into government, residential, and commercial areas. The resulting districts still exist as the Colonial District, Chinatown, and Kampong Glam. In the Colonial District, most government buildings surrounding the Padang have been converted into arts venues.

Statue of Raffles

This bronze statue of Sir Stamford Raffles was erected at the Padang in 1887, and it was moved to its current location outside the Victoria Theatre and Concert Hall in 1919, to mark Singapore's first centennial. A replica is perched at the spot along the Singapore River where it is believed that Raffles first set foot on the island in 1819.
⚜ Map M3 • 9 Empress Place

Raffles Hotel

The Colonial District has been the location of numerous hotels for European visitors, but only one stands today. Raffles Hotel was built from an existing bungalow in 1887, and after extensions and renovations, has grown into an iconic landmark. W. Somerset Maugham, a frequent guest since the 1920s, commented that the hotel stood for "all the fables of the exotic East" (see pp24–5).

City Hall and the Supreme Court

Since its completion in 1929, City Hall has been the site of many historical events. In 1945 the Japanese surrendered here; in 1959 Prime Minister Lee Kuan Yew proclaimed Singapore's self-rule on the steps; and in 1966 it was the site of Singapore's first National Day celebrations. The Supreme Court was built in 1932, and while both buildings are massive, the government has outgrown them. The judiciary now operates from the new Supreme Court building behind the original one, while the City Hall offices now occupy other modern buildings. ⚜ Map M2, M3
• St. Andrew's Rd. • No public access

The City Hall and Supreme Court buildings

8 National Museum of Singapore

The largest museum in Singapore, the National Museum has over 194 sq ft (18,000 sq m) of exhibit space, with galleries dedicated to presenting Singapore's history and heritage through entertaining multimedia displays. This is a highly recommended introduction to Singapore *(see pp8–9)*.

Gallery at the Philatelic Museum

9 Singapore Art Museum

Though small, this museum of contemporary arts is the largest in the region and is an important pillar for the Southeast Asian arts community. Dedicated to preserving Southeast Asia's representative arts, the museum focuses on encouraging art awareness through exhibitions and programs. ◈ *Map L1, M1*
• *71 Bras Basah Rd.* • *6332-3222* • *Open 10am–7pm Sat–Thu, 10am–9pm Fri* • *Adm (free noon–2pm Mon–Fri, after 6pm Fri)*
• *www.singart.com*

10 Singapore Philatelic Museum

This museum documents Singapore's history and heritage through its own collection of rare stamps, as well as those on loan from private collectors. Visiting exhibits display stamp collections from around Southeast Asia. ◈ *Map L2* • *23B Coleman Street* • *6337-3888* • *Open 9am–7pm Tue–Sun, 1–7pm Mon* • *Adm* • *www.spm.org.sg*

A Walk Around the Colonial District

Morning

Begin at the **National Museum** *(see pp8–9)*, where you can spend a few hours exploring the history of Singapore. From here, turn right onto Stamford Road and walk as far as Armenian Street to your right. Along Armenian Street you will find the **Peranakan Museum** *(see p36)*, which explores the culture of the Peranakans, or Straits Chinese. Continue along Armenian Street until you reach the intersection with Victoria Street where the **Funan – DigitaLife Mall** *(see p49)* is located. Here you'll find an array of electronic goods, including computer hardware and software.

Afternoon

After lunch, exit the Funan Mall from North Bridge Road and turn left. At the intersection of North Bridge Road and Bras Basah Road turn left into **CHIJMES** *(see p35)*, a 19th-century missionary school, which is now a dining and shopping area. Back at the intersection, cross to **Raffles Hotel** for a tour of this landmark. Exit from its main entrance on Beach Road, turn right and continue as far as **St. Andrew's Cathedral** *(see p38)* beside City Hall MRT. After visiting the chapel, follow the road with the Padang to your left and the **Supreme Court** to your right. Walk past the **Old Parliament House** *(see pp10–11)* and **Victoria Theatre** *(see p85)* on your right to the **Empress Place Building** to spend the rest of your day exploring the **Asian Civilisations Museum** *(see pp10–11)*.

Left **Raffles Gift Shop** Center **Gold-plated orchid by RISIS** Right **Royal Selangor pewter**

TOP 10 Shopping

1 Bugis Street Night Market
Contrary to its name, the stalls here are open both day and night, selling souvenirs and cheap accessories. ◎ *Map G6 • Parco Bugis Junction, Victoria St. • Open 2–11pm daily (some stalls open 10am)*

2 Olathe
A collection of modern ladies' clothing by batik designer Peter Hoe, plus textiles, wood-carvings, and jewelry from around Southeast Asia. ◎ *Map M1 • #01–05 CHIJMES, 30 Victoria St. • 6339-6880 • Open 10am–8pm daily*

3 Raffles Gift Shop
Find every kind of gift, from T-shirts to bone china, bearing the Raffles emblem. ◎ *Map M1 • Raffles Hotel, 1 Beach Rd. • 6337-1886 • Open 8:30am–8:30pm daily*

4 Cathay Photo
This camera store offers quality stock at bargain prices. ◎ *Map L2 • Peninsula Plaza, 111 North Bridge Rd. • 6337-4274 • Open 10am–7pm Mon–Sat*

5 ARTrium@MICA
Private galleries specializing in the contemporary art of Asia surround the atrium lobby of this government building *(see p47)*.

6 RISIS
In 1976, a Singapore government agency developed a way to preserve an orchid in 24-carat gold. Now, RISIS sells jewelry pieces made from the national orchid, the Vanda Miss Joaquim, and other varieties. ◎ *Map M1 • Suntec City Tower 1, 3 Temasek Blvd. • 6338-8250 • Open 11am–9pm daily*

7 Challenger
This megastore offers computer accessories at great prices. ◎ *Map L2 • Funan DigitaLife Mall, 109 North Bridge Rd. • 6339-9008 • Open 10:30am–8pm Sun–Fri, 10:30am–9pm Sat*

8 Royal Selangor Pewter Centre
Established in 1885, this has a reputation for selling fine pewter goods. ◎ *Map K2 • 3A River Valley Rd. • 6268-9600 • Open 9am–9pm daily*

9 Museum Shop by Banyan Tree
For "green" gifts, books, and spa products by Banyan Tree resorts. ◎ *Map M3 • Asian Civilisations Museum, 1 Empress Place Ave. • 6336-9050 • Open 9am–7pm Tue–Thu & Sun, 9am–9pm Fri, 1–7pm Mon*

10 The Planet Traveller
For travel gear, books, maps, and even luggage repair. ◎ *Map N3 • 6 Raffles Boulevard • 6337-0291 • Open 10:30am–9pm daily*

Price Categories

For a three-course meal for one with a non-alchoholic drink (or equivalent meal), taxes, and extra charges.

$	under S$20
$$	S$20–30
$$$	S$30–50
$$$$	S$50–70
$$$$$	over S$70

Left **Lei Garden at CHIJMES**

🔟 Restaurants

1 Rendezvous Restaurant
The 60-year history of this place is evident in its old-world decor. Cuisine is authentic *nasi padang*. ◎ *Map F5 • Hotel Rendezvous, 9 Bras Basah Rd. • 6339-7508 • Open 11am–9pm daily • $*

2 Equinox
Great views and fine dining in Southeast Asia's tallest hotel. ◎ *Map M2 • Swissôtel, 2 Stamford Rd. • 6837-3322 • Open noon–2.30pm, 3–5pm & 6:30–11pm Mon–Sat, 11am–2:30pm & 7–11pm Sun • $$$$$*

3 Lei Garden
Enjoy authentic Cantonese cuisine in a dining room within the historic CHIJMES complex. The dim sum is delicious. ◎ *Map M1 • 30 Victoria St. • 6339-3822 • Open 11:30am–3pm & 6–11pm daily • $$$$*

4 Tiffin Room
This Asian restaurant is named for the 3-tiered Indian lunchbox. ◎ *Map M1 • 1 Beach Rd. • 6331-1612 • Open 7–10am, 3:30–5:30pm & 7–10pm daily, noon–2pm Mon–Sat, 11:30am–2:30pm Sun • $$$$*

5 My Humble House
The sleek interior is the perfect setting for the innovative Chinese haute cuisine. ◎ *Map N3 • 8 Raffles Avenue • 6423-1881 • Open 11:45am–3pm, 6:30–11pm daily • $$$$$*

6 Quayside Seafood
This alfresco eatery, with views of the Singapore River, serves fresh local-style seafood.

◎ *Map K2 • 3A River Valley Rd., Clarke Quay • 6434-5288 • Open 6pm–midnight Sun–Thu, 6pm–1am Fri–Sat • $$$*

7 Prego
A colorful bistro appealing to locals and tourists. The thin-crust pizzas are superb. ◎ *Map M1 • 80 Bras Basah Rd. • 6431-6156 • Open 11:30am–2:30pm Mon–Sat, noon–2:30pm Sun, 6:30–10:30pm daily • $$$*

8 Soup Restaurant
This restaurant serves old-fashioned Chinese recipes and the soups are a must. ◎ *Map M1 • 39 Seah St. • 6333-9388 • Open 11:30am–2:30pm & 5:30–10pm daily • $$*

9 Flutes at the Fort
Specializing in contemporary Australian food, Flutes serves a perfect rack of lamb. ◎ *Map L1 • 21 Lewin Terrace • 6338-8770 • Open noon–2pm & 6:30–10pm Mon–Fri, 11am–2:30pm & 6:30–10:30pm Sat • $$$$$*

10 Sage The Restaurant
Enjoy melt-in-your-mouth variations of classic French food. ◎ *Map J2 • 7 Mohammed Sultan Rd. • 6333-8726 • Open noon–2:30pm Wed–Fri, 6:30–10:30pm Tue–Sun • $$$*

Left **Crossroads Café** Center **Goodwood Park Hotel** Right **Row houses on Emerald Hill Road**

Orchard Road

ORCHARD ROAD GETS ITS NAME *from the plantations that sprouted here in the 1830s at a time when nutmeg was an important cash crop, along with fruits, spices, and pepper. By the mid-1800s, the nutmeg plantations had been wiped out by disease. Around the same time, the European population grew larger, demanding more space. Orchard Road cut through a narrow valley and suffered terrible floods, but once drainage plans were in place, businesses settled in the area to serve the colonial expatriate community. In 1958, C.K. Tang opened the first store here, and by 1973 Orchard Road had its first skyscraper, the Mandarin Hotel, now Meritus Mandarin Singapore, with a revolving restaurant on its 39th floor offering views of the entire area.*

Ngee Ann City mall

🔟 Sights

1. The Istana and Sri Temasek
2. Emerald Hill Road
3. Singapore Botanic Gardens
4. Tangs
5. Tanglin Mall
6. Ngee Ann City
7. Goodwood Park Hotel
8. Crossroads Café
9. Street Performances
10. Youth Park and Skate Park

1 The Istana and Sri Temasek

The Istana was considered expensive for a governor's residence, but upon completion in 1869, its design won critics over. Situated at the top of a hill, it is surrounded by tropical gardens. The Istana no longer serves as a residence, but is used for state occasions, VIP receptions, and is open to visitors on public holidays. Sri Temasek, a smaller building in the compound, was built for colonial officers *(see p35)*.

2 Emerald Hill Road

Away from the cacophony of Orchard Road, Emerald Hill Road is surprisingly tranquil. A lane of millionaires' homes have been well restored. There are various house styles, from plain, boxy 19th-century buildings, to the pre-war Chinese Baroque-style terrace houses, and even ornate Art Deco variations of the 1950s shophouse. *Map C4–5*

3 Singapore Botanic Gardens

These lovely gardens remind visitors of the area's agricultural origins, and remind residents that the city was once covered in

Entrance to the Singapore Botanic Gardens

lush tropical forest. The gardens are a favorite spot for joggers in the mornings, for photographers in the late afternoons, and for families on the weekends, who come for the Jacob Balas Children's Garden. There are also music and dance performances, and movie screenings by the lakes *(see pp18–19)*.

4 Tangs

Singapore's home grown department store sprouted from the dreams of a door-to-door salesman who arrived from China in 1923. Called the "Tin Trunk Man," C.K. Tang carried goods in a tin trunk that became his trademark. Tang bought this prime piece of property in 1958 to be near the European settlements in the area. His family still owns the department store and the plot of land on which it sits, located at the city's busiest crossroads. *Map B4 • 310 & 320 Orchard Rd. • 6737-5500 • Open 10:30am–9:30pm Mon–Thu, 10:30am–11pm Fri–Sat, 11am–8:30pm Sun • www.tangs.com*

The Scotts Road entrance to Tangs Department Store

A shopping street near Tanglin Mall

Tanglin Mall

Known as an expat enclave, Tanglin Mall is a popular place for expatriates to shop for imported groceries and special goods. Most foreigners spotted here will be from around the world. The US and UK embassies and the British Council are across the street. ◈ *Map S3 • Tanglin Rd.*

Ngee Ann City

Owned by the Ngee Ann Kongsi group, this spectacular shopping mall is designed like a city-within-a-city. Its Oriental façade complements the Western interior to create a unique cosmopolitan ambience, and makes a majestic statement along Orchard Road. Its largest tenant is Takashimaya, a retail giant in Japan. The mall houses more than 30 international restaurants. Book lovers can browse an extensive selection at Asia's largest bookstore, Kinokuniya Singapore. ◈ *Map B4, B5, C4, C5 • 391 Orchard Rd. • 6506-0461*
• Open 10am–9:30pm daily
• www.ngeeanncity.com.sg

The Stamford Canal

Orchard Road's pedestrian mall sits above a huge canal that drains storm water, protecting the entire area from flash floods during monsoon downpours. The Stamford Canal begins at Tanglin Road, runs underneath Wisma Atria and Ngee Ann City, and continues all the way past City Hall and into Marina Bay.

Goodwood Park Hotel

Built in 1900, this hotel began as the Teutonia Club – an enclave for expatriate Germans. In 1929 it turned into Goodwood Park Hotel, for businessmen from Malaya. It has withstood both World Wars, and much of the original beauty – fluted columns, delicate woodwork, decorative plasterwork, and graceful archways – have been faithfully restored. The six restaurants here, including Min Jiang, L'Espresso, and Coffee Lounge, have all swept awards. ◈ *Map B3 • 22 Scotts Rd. • 6737-7411 • www.goodwoodparkhotel.com*

Crossroads Café

The city's best spot for people-watching, this alfresco café sits at Singapore's busiest intersection between Orchard, Scotts, and Paterson Roads. The sidewalks teem with hordes of

The atrium at Orchard Cineleisure

bustling shoppers. Virtually every tourist passes this spot, as do locals who come to Orchard Road for the malls, teenagers who flock here to hang out and, on weekends, maids who gather to catch up with friends on their day off. ✆ Map B4 • Singapore Marriott Hotel, 320 Orchard Rd. • 6831-4605 • 6am–11pm daily • www.crossroads.singaporemarriott.com

A street performer on Orchard Road

Street Performances

Singapore has recently liberalized public performance regulations, paving the way for street musicians, comedians, and magicians. Various international busker festivals invite some of the world's best street performers to work the crowds. Orchard Road has recently widened its sidewalks and added special performance areas for buskers. The tourism board (see p107) provides information about planned busker events. ✆ Map A4–C4, C5–E5 • Orchard Rd.

Youth Park and Skate Park

These two parks, along with neighboring Orchard Cineleisure and Heeren Shopping Mall, attract young locals with free concerts, carnivals, and gigs. The skate park hums into the night, while the movie theater at Cineleisure screens midnight movies on weekends. ✆ Map C5

A Stroll Along Orchard Road

Morning

Start at the Orchard Road Promenade and head to **Ngee Ann City**, which has some of the world's most luxurious brands. Shop for books at the city's largest bookstore, **Kinokuniya Singapore** (see p94), and inspect handcrafted batiks from Indonesia at **Bin House** (see p94). From **Ngee Ann City** follow the promenade past street buskers and resting spots. On your left is **Tangs** department store, next to **Lucky Plaza**, known for cheap electronic goods – but beware, some stores will take advantage of tourists. On your right, pass the **Meritus Mandarin Hotel Singapore**, known for its chicken rice. Farther down Orchard Road is the Heeren shopping mall on your left and **Orchard Cineleisure** on your right. Continue along Orchard Road to the junction at **Peranakan Place** on your left. This nook has many cafés and watering holes.

Afternoon

Walk past Peranakan Place to **Emerald Hill Road** to view the private homes converted from Peranakan shophouses. A few of these are now pubs and stores, where you can see inside. No. 5 has retained many original details. Walk back to **Orchard Road** and continue along the promenade. Detours into its malls can easily occupy most of your day. On public holidays, the late afternoon is the best time to visit **The Istana and Sri Temasek** (see p91), which is located past the intersection with Clemenceau Avenue.

Left **Atrium at DFS Galleria** Right **Hilton Shopping Gallery**

Shopping

1 Tangs
Singapore's homegrown department store, Tangs offers a broad range of international and local fashions *(see p91)*.

2 Takashimaya
One of Japan's oldest and largest retailers, this huge store stocks apparel, cosmetics, and household items. ◎ *Map B4 • 391 Orchard Rd. • 6738-1111 • Open 10am–9:30pm daily*

3 Hilton Shopping Gallery
Though compact, this hotel gallery hosts the biggest luxury brands, including Bvlgari, Dolce & Gabbana, Giorgio Armani, and Cartier. ◎ *Map A4 • 581 Orchard Rd. • 6734-5250 • Open 10am–6pm daily*

4 Kinokuniya Singapore
With more than 500,000 titles, this quality bookstore has the city's largest collection of retail books. ◎ *Map B4 • 03–10/15 Takashimaya • 6737-5021 • Open 10am–9:30pm Sun–Fri, 10am–10pm Sat*

5 Naga Arts & Antiques
With furniture from Tibet, Buddha images from Burma, and textiles from China, Naga promises a terrific rummage opportunity for bargain-hunters. ◎ *Map A4 • 19 Tanglin Rd. • 6235-7084 • Open 10:30am–6:30pm Mon–Sat*

6 Shanghai Tang
A luxury brand featuring clothing inspired by China's fashion heritage, which mixes some traditional designs with vivid colors. ◎ *Map B4 • #02/12 Takashimaya • 6737-3537 • Open 10:30am–8:30pm Mon–Sat, 11am–8:30pm Sun*

7 Mumbai Se
India's textile heritage is converted into colorful, ethnic-inspired high fashion. ◎ *Map A4 • 390 Orchard Rd. • 6733-7188 • Open 10:30am–8pm Mon–Sat, 11am–7pm Sun*

8 Bin House
Indonesia's cloth-weaving and batik-dye techniques are showcased in the handcrafted sarongs, scarves, and shawls here. ◎ *Map B4 • #02–12F Takashimaya • 6733-6789 • Open 11am–9pm daily*

9 Hassan's Carpets
One of Singapore's oldest family-run businesses, Hassan's Carpets boasts quality and artistic integrity. ◎ *Map A4 • #01–12/13 19 Tanglin Rd. • 6737-5626 • Open 10am–7pm Mon–Sat, 11am–4pm Sun*

10 DFS Galleria
The world's largest duty-free luxury goods retailer delivers purchases to the airport. ◎ *Map B4 • 25 Scotts Rd. • 6229-8100 • Open 10am–10pm Sun–Thu, 10am–10:30pm Fri–Sat*

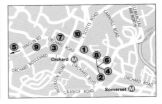

Price Categories

For a three-course meal for one with a non-alchoholic drink (or equivalent meal), taxes, and extra charges.

$	under S$20
$$	S$20–30
$$$	S$30–50
$$$$	S$50–70
$$$$$	over S$70

Left **The Rice Table**

🔟 Restaurants

1 Les Amis
The creative contemporary European menu here has won countless awards. ✧ *Map B4 • 1 Scotts Rd. • 6733-2225 • Open noon–2:30pm & 7–10:30pm Mon–Sat • $$$$$*

2 Crystal Jade Palace
This flagship restaurant of the Crystal Jade chain serves Cantonese-style dishes. ✧ *Map B4 • 04–19 391 Orchard Rd. • 6735-2388 • Open 11:30am–11pm Mon–Fri, 11:30am–3pm & 6–11pm Sat–Sun • $$$$*

3 The Line
A buffet of 16 food stations serves tandoori, sushi, meats, salads, stirfrys, and pasta. ✧ *Map A3 • Shangri-La Hotel, 22 Orange Grove Rd. • 6213-4275 • Open 6–10:30am, noon–2:30pm & 6:30pm–6am daily • $$$$*

4 mezza9
This Grand Hyatt restaurant offers nine dining experiences, including a martini and cigar bar and a European deli. ✧ *Map B4 • Grand Hyatt, 10 Scotts Rd. • 6416-7189 • Open noon–11pm Mon–Sat, 11:30am–11pm Sun • $$$$$*

5 StraitsKitchen
Diners at this open-kitchen restaurant watch chefs prepare fresh Asian dishes. ✧ *Map B4 • Grand Hyatt, 10 Scotts Rd. • 6732-1234 • Open 6:30am–midnight daily • $$$*

6 The Sanctuary
This alfresco café and lounge serves Vietnamese, Laotian, Cambodian, and Western food. ✧ *Map B4 • 435 Orchard Rd. • 6238-3473 • Open noon–2am Mon–Thu, noon–3am Fri–Sat, noon–1am Sun • $$$*

7 Tandoor North Indian Restaurant
An award-winning place serving Singapore's best northern Indian food. ✧ *Map D5 • Holiday Inn Parkview, 11 Cavenagh Rd. • 6730-0153 • Open noon–2:30pm & 7–10:30pm daily • $$$$*

8 Patara Fine Thai
Authentic Thai food is complemented by specialties combining Thai and Western flavors. ✧ *163 Tanglin Rd. • 6737-0818 • Open noon–3pm & 6–10pm daily • $$$*

9 The Rice Table
Here you can enjoy *rijsttafel* – Indonesian-style meats, seafood, and vegetables served with different rice dishes. ✧ *Map B4 • 02–09 International Building 360 Orchard Rd. • 6835-3783 • Open noon–3pm & 6–9:15pm daily • $$*

10 Chatterbox
This revolving restaurant is famous for chicken rice, a local favorite. ✧ *Map C5 • 333 Orchard Rd. • 6831-6291 • Open 5–1am Sun–Thu, 24 hrs Fri–Sat • $$$*

Left **Sungei Buloh Wetland Reserve** Right **Bukit Timah Nature Reserve**

Farther Afield

SHAPED LIKE A DIAMOND, SINGAPORE is only 7,349 sq ft (683 sq m) in size with 120 miles (193 km) of shoreline. The urban center sits at the southernmost tip of the island. At the city's outskirts, pre-war neighborhoods consist of low-rise streets with homes and stores where traditional trades are still practiced. Beyond these, New Towns – clusters of high-rise apartment buildings – are supported by schools, businesses, and other facilities. The Mass Rapid Transit line (RMT) runs a full circle around the major New Towns, linking them with the city. It is possible to spend several days exploring the vast countryside.

10 Sights

1 Singapore Zoo and Night Safari

2 Jurong BirdPark

3 Bukit Timah Nature Reserve

4 Chinese and Japanese Gardens

5 Sungei Buloh Wetland Reserve

6 Sun Yat Sen Nanyang Memorial Hall

7 Lian Shan Shuang Lin Temple

8 The Southern Ridges

9 Mandai Orchid Garden

10 Kranji War Memorial and Cemetery

The twin pagodas at the Chinese and Japanese Gardens

1 Singapore Zoo and Night Safari

A must-see attraction, the zoo has exotic animals in landscaped enclosures, a playground for children, scheduled feeding times, guided tours, and animal shows. The Night Safari is the world's first, and a novel way to see nocturnal animals at their most active. Located next to the Mandai Reservoir, the zoo attracts many local animals, such

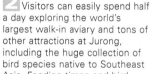
White tiger at Singapore Zoo

as monitor lizards and macaques, that wander in from the surrounding jungle for free meals *(see pp8–9)*.

2 Jurong BirdPark

Visitors can easily spend half a day exploring the world's largest walk-in aviary and tons of other attractions at Jurong, including the huge collection of bird species native to Southeast Asia. Feeding times and bird shows are scheduled throughout the day, including the early morning breakfast show, when the birds are full of song and the day still cool. ❧ *Map R2 • 2 Jurong Hill • 6265-0022 • Open 8:30am–6pm daily • Adm • www.birdpark.com.sg*

3 Bukit Timah Nature Reserve

A rare chance to experience primary rain forest within a city, this large nature preserve has five hiking trails that range from easy walks to more challenging hikes, most taking 2 hours to complete. The park is home to a variety of birds, insects, and small

mammals. It adheres to conservation acts to protect its biodiversity and prohibits activities that may disturb the flora and fauna, such as feeding the animals or biking off designated paths. The visitors' center provides information to help guests navigate their way, as well as restrooms, public telephones, and a first-aid station. ❧ *Map S2 • 177 Hindhede Drive • 6468-5736 • Open 8:30am–6:30pm daily • www. nparks.gov.sg*

4 Chinese and Japanese Gardens

Designed to resemble an imperial garden, the arched bridges, moon gates, and twin pagodas of the Chinese Garden blend with bamboo groves, trees, and flowering shrubs. A Suzhou-style courtyard provides a serene backdrop for the garden's collection of bonsai. A stone boat and teahouse grace a calm lake. In comparison, the adjoining Japanese Garden has a minimalist Zen feel, with pebble paths and landscaping to evoke a sense of contemplation. ❧ *Map R2 • 1 Chinese Garden Rd. • 6261-3632 • Open 9am–6pm daily • Adm (for the Garden of Abundance in Chinese Garden)*

Feeding time at Jurong BirdPark

The Garden City

Over 40 years ago, then Prime Minister Lee Kuan Yew recognized the value of nature. By the 1970s, several areas had been planted with shady angsana trees and bougainvilleas. Since then, new urban plans have continued to be drawn up with nature in mind. The National Parks Board manages 23,475 acres (9,500 ha) in more than 300 parks.

5 Sungei Buloh Wetland Reserve

A series of paths and wooden walkways leads visitors through mangrove swamps, mudflats, and pools, overgrown with the unique flowers and foliage that thrive at the edge of the sea. Kingfishers, plovers, sandpipers, egrets, and herons are just some of the bird species found here. Other wildlife includes otters, crabs, and mud lobsters. The visitors' center shows a film featuring information on the park's history. ◈ Map R1 • 301 Neo Tiew Crescent • 6794-1401 • Open 7:30am–7pm Mon–Sat, 7am–7pm Sun • Adm (Sat & Sun) • www.sbwr.org.sg

6 Sun Yat Sen Nanyang Memorial Hall

This 19th-century suburban bungalow was a private residence before it was donated by a local businessman to Chinese revolutionary Dr. Sun Yat Sen for use as the headquarters of his operations in Southeast Asia. In 1911, after Dr. Sun's Kuomintang Party deposed China's Qing dynasty, it was entrusted to the local Chinese Chamber of Commerce. The bungalow is now a museum tracing the history of Dr. Sun's revolution and the contributions made by Chinese of the Nanyang, or South Sea, to his cause. ◈ Map T2 • 12 Tai Gin Rd. • 6256-7377 • Open 9am–5pm Tue–Sun • Adm • www.wanqingyuan.com.sg

7 Lian Shan Shuang Lin Temple

Singapore's oldest Buddhist monastery, whose name means "Twin Grove of the Lotus Mountain Temple," claims a 110-year history. It has three main halls – the Hall of Celestial Kings, the Mahavira Hall, and the Dharma Hall. Each of these is built in the typical architectural style of China's southern Fujian province. The compound has a seven-story granite pagoda. The local Hokkiens call this temple Siong Lim in their dialect. ◈ Map T2 • 184 Jalan Toa Payoh • 6259-6924 • Open 24 hours daily

8 The Southern Ridges

The coastline along the island's southwest shore is fringed by hills and slopes with rocky ridges. Four parks – Mount Faber Park, Telok Blangah Hill Park, Kent Ridge Park, and West

Sun Yat Sen Nanyang Memorial Hall

Mandai Orchid Garden

Coast Park – are seamlessly connected by a series of bridges that link hiking trails. The views here are superb, especially from the dramatic Henderson Waves bridge, a causeway connecting Mount Faber and Telok Blangah Hill parks. ◉ *Map S3* • *Henderson Rd.* • *1800-471-7300* • *Open 24 hours daily* • *www.nparks.goc.sg*

9 Mandai Orchid Garden
Best visited in conjunction with the Singapore Zoo, this commercial garden grows more than 200 varieties of orchid for local sale and export, as well as other cut flowers, tropical fruits, herbs, and spices. There are also a café and a restaurant in the grounds. ◉ *Map S1* • *200 Mandai Lake Rd.* • *6269-1036* • *Open 9am–6pm daily* • *Adm* • *www.mandai.com.sg*

10 Kranji War Memorial and Cemetery
This serene cemetery, overlooking the Strait of Johor, is lined by 4,000 tombstones that mark the graves of the British, Australians, Canadians, Indians, and Malays who lost their lives during World War II. A memorial is dedicated to 24,000 soldiers whose remains were never recovered. ◉ *Map R1* • *9 Woodlands Rd.* • *Open 7am–6pm daily*

A Day Trip from Singapore

Morning

🕐 Register in advance for a GT one-day pass (www.bushub.com.sg), which permits unlimited travel between major attractions for S$11 per adult. Take an early Express Service bus from one of the stops on Orchard Road to the **Singapore Zoo** *(see pp20–21)*. Take advantage of the cooler morning hours to tour the zoo while the animals are more active. Next, hop on public bus #138 for the five-minute trip to the **Mandai Orchid Garden** to explore its winding green trails between hundreds of beds of flowering plants.

Afternoon

Have lunch at The Vanilla Pod restaurant at the Mandai Orchid Garden, where chefs prepare dishes using fresh orchids as well as other herbs and spices cultivated on the site. Both the air-conditioned dining room and the veranda offer refreshing views of the gardens. After lunch, hop on bus #138 back to the zoo, and board the Express Service bus to **Jurong BirdPark** *(see p97)* in western Singapore. You could spend a whole afternoon touring the grounds on the panorail, exploring the Waterfall Aviary, learning about native species, and taking in one of the animal behavior shows. Another great option for the afternoon is a visit to the **Chinese and Japanese Gardens** *(see p97)*, a taxi ride away. Its picturesque bridges, lakes, pagodas, and bonsai are wonderfully photogenic.

Left **Shophouses in Katong** Right **The modern town of Pasir Ris**

Suburban Neighborhoods

1 Katong/Joo Chiat
A melting-pot of Peranakan, Eurasian, Malay, Indian, and Chinese cultures, these are two areas that promise a treasure trove of food stalls. ⊗ *Map T2*

2 Geylang
While Kampong Glam captures the diversity of the city's Muslim culture, Geylang is Malay-influenced. The stores and eateries here target locals rather than tourists, so it has a genuinely Malay feel. ⊗ *Map T2*

3 Siglap
A quiet residential neighborhood, Siglap has become popular with expatriates. Some nice restaurants and cafés, known for their laid-back feel, have sprouted up here. ⊗ *Map U2*

4 Tiong Bahru
One of Singapore's oldest New Towns, Tiong Bahru has preserved its art deco buildings. It is also turning into a hub for creative artists, offering a blend of old and new. The hawker center is a must. ⊗ *Map S3*

5 Holland Village
Singapore's original expatriate enclave has some interesting Asian art, besides stores selling gifts and home furnishings. With some trendy sidewalk cafés and bars, too, it appeals to residents of various nationalities who rub shoulders here every day. ⊗ *Map S2–3*

6 Dempsey Road
A cluster of former military barracks close to the Botanic Gardens, Dempsey Hill offers one-stop shopping for art, antiques, carpets, and home decor. The area's cafés, bars, and restaurants are popular on weekends and evenings. ⊗ *Map S2*

7 Toa Payoh
A prime example of a New Town, Toa Payoh is centrally located, surrounded by high-rise housing flats, with a bustling mall that serves the local community. Many of the stores have been here for decades. ⊗ *Map T2*

8 Changi Point
This rural seaside village has an open-air hawker center, golf course, a good beach for watersports, and a ferry launch where you can pick up boats to Pulau Ubin island. ⊗ *Map V1*

9 Woodlands
Singapore's last town before reaching Malaysia, Woodlands has one of the largest shopping malls in the city, as well as a big American community that has settled here near the Singapore American School. ⊗ *Map S1*

10 Pasir Ris
A modern New Town, Pasir Ris is located by the sea, with beaches, watersports, waterfront parks, family activities, and alfresco hawker centers and restaurants. ⊗ *Map U1, U2*

Price Categories

For a three-course meal for one with a non-alcholoic drink (or equivalent meal), taxes, and extra charges.	**$** under S$20
	$$ S$20–30
	$$$ S$30–50
	$$$$ S$50–70
	$$$$$ over S$70

Left **Open-air dining at UDMC Food Centre**

TOP 10 Restaurants

1 UDMC Food Centre
Fun for its breezy waterfront ambience, this cluster of open-air restaurants offers fresh seafood. ❧ *Map U3 • 1202 East Coast Parkway • Open 11am–midnight daily • $$$*

2 Long Beach Seafood
Famed for its Sri Lankan crabs in black pepper sauce, Long Beach also serves great meat dishes. ❧ *Map U3 • 1018 East Coast Parkway • 6445-8833 • Open 11am–3pm & 5pm–12:15am Mon–Fri, 11am–1am Sat & public holidays, 11am–midnight Sun • $$$*

3 Samy's Curry Restaurant
Visit this Indian coffee shop, occupying an open-air hall amid trees, for its signature chicken masala. ❧ *Map S3 • 25 Dempsey Rd. • 6472-2080 • Open 11:30am–3pm & 6–10pm daily • $*

4 Original Sin
Here you can enjoy light Mediterranean vegetarian food enhanced with fresh ingredients and herbs, all complemented by fine wines. ❧ *Map S3 • 43 Jalan Merah Saga • 6475-5605 • Open 11:30am–2:30pm & 6–10:30pm Tue–Sat, 6–10pm Sun • $$$*

5 Siem Reap I
A chic café adorned by replicas of Cambodian temple friezes and Buddha images. It features cuisine from Vietnam, Laos, and Cambodia. ❧ *Map S3 • 44 Lorong Mambong • 6468-5798 • Open 1pm–1am daily (cocktails 3–6pm) • $$$*

6 Halia
This glass and thatch house is nestled within lush foliage. The menu offers mainly Western dishes that have local touches. ❧ *Map S2 • 1 Cluny Rd. • 6476-6711 • Open 2–11pm Mon–Fri, 9am–11pm Sat–Sun • $$$$*

7 Imperial Herbal
Guests here undergo a brief check-up from the resident Chinese physician, who prescribes the appropriate herbal ingredients to be added to the dishes they order. ❧ *Map S3 • #03–08 VivoCity • 6337-0491 • Open 11:30am–2:15pm & 6:15–10:15pm daily • $$$$*

8 Bistro Petit Salut
A top choice for French cuisine, this restaurant prepares classic dishes with authenticity. It has an elegant dining room and an alfresco area popular with expatriates. ❧ *Map S3 • 44 Jalan Merah Saga • 6475-1976 • Open 11:30am–2:30pm & 6:30–10:30pm Mon–Sat • $$$$*

9 Chilli Padi
This award-winning eatery offers a selection of Peranakan favorites – a unique type of Straits Chinese cuisine. ❧ *Map T2 • 11 Joo Chiat Place • 6275-1002 • Open 11am–2:30pm & 5:30–10pm daily • $$$*

10 Vansh
Dine under the stars on fine northern Indian fare at the Kallang River waterfront. ❧ *Map T3 • 2 Stadium Walk • 6345-4466 • Open noon–2:30pm & 6–10pm daily • $$$$*

Recommend your favorite restaurant on **traveldk.com**

STREETSMART

SINGAPORE'S TOP 10

Left **Local currency** Center **Hat, sunglasses, and sunblock** Right **Electrical plug**

TOP 10 Planning Your Trip

1 When to Go
Singapore's temperature remains fairly constant throughout the year, with an average high of 88°F (31°C) and relative humidity of 85 percent. Rainfall is highest from November to January and lowest in June and July. Peak travel season is from mid-December through to the Chinese New Year in January/February.

2 Passports and Visas
Visitors to Singapore require a passport that is valid for at least six months, evidence of sufficient funds for their stay, and documents for onward travel. Western nationals do not require a visa and are issued a social visit pass of up to 30 days on arrival. Women who are over six months pregnant need to apply for a social visit pass before arrival; these can be obtained through local embassies or the Immigration and Checkpoints Authority.
⊗ ICA • 6391-6100
• www.ica.gov.sg

3 Health Precautions
There are no mandatory vaccinations but it is recommended that visitors have up-to-date hepatitis A & B, diphtheria, tetanus, and typhoid shots. Customs regulations are strict – you may need to show your doctor's prescription if you are using any sleeping pills, stimulants, or depressants.

4 Customs
Duty-free allowance is 1 liter of spirits, 1 liter of wine or port, and 1 liter of beer. No duty-free cigarettes can be brought into Singapore. There is no duty-free allowance for visitors from Malaysia or those out of Singapore for less than 48 hours. Firecrackers, pirated CDs/DVDs, and chewing gum are all banned items. The city's mandatory death sentence for drug offenses applies to foreigners too.

5 What to Pack
Pack light summer wear. Locals dress in western casuals, though some restaurants may frown upon shorts or sandals. Carry a jacket or shawl for air-conditioned places, and an umbrella to protect you from both sun and rain.

6 Time Zone
Singapore is 8 hours ahead of GMT, 13 hours ahead of New York, and 3 hours behind Sydney. There is no daylight savings time; sunrise and sunset are around 7am and 7pm all year.

7 Electricity
Singapore's electrical voltage is modeled on the British system of 220–240 volts. Power plugs are also of the British three-pin type. Transformers are available and hotels have a supply to loan guests.

8 Languages
There are four official languages in Singapore. These are English, Mandarin, Malay, and Tamil. English is the most commonly used language and is taught in all schools. However, many Singaporeans also tend to use "Singlish" slang terms in their casual conversation (see p33). Public notices and signs are all in English.

9 Currency
The Singapore dollar (SGD) is divided into 100 cents. Notes come in denominations of S$2, S$5, S$10, S$20, S$50, and up to S$10,000. Coins come in 1, 5, 10, 20, 50 cent, and S$1 denominations. Although some stores accept British, US, Brunei, or Australian currency, you will find that SGD is needed for most transactions.

10 Driver's Licenses
Visitors intending to drive in Singapore require a valid driver's license from their country of residence, an English translation of their own license document, or an International Driving Permit. ⊗ www.driving-in-singapore.spf.gov.sg

Left **Airplanes at Changi Airport** Right **Travel agent making a flight reservation**

TOP 10 Getting to Singapore

1 Direct Flights
Changi Airport is a major hub, and with more than 80 airlines flying into Singapore, most travelers enjoy a wide choice of airlines, fares, and schedules. There are frequent direct flights to major cities including London, New York, Paris, and Sydney.

2 Stopovers
Singapore Visitors Centre offices, located in terminal arrivals, suggest activities for stopovers. Depending on the length of stopover, passengers can make use of napping areas, transit hotels, spas, and even a rooftop pool at Terminal 1. Free English-language tours are available for all passengers with a stopover of more than 5 hours, subject to entry visa regulations.

3 Flight Booking Tips
The best deals are often available online and many airlines offer Internet-only fares on their websites. Some sites, such as Kayak or Travelocity, send email alerts for tickets below a target price. Buying very early or late can net good results. ◈ www.kayak.com; www.travelocity.com

4 Regional Budget Carriers
The global expansion of low-cost airlines has served Singapore well, and several carriers such as Tiger Airways, JetStar, and Air Asia offer budget flights across the Asia Pacific region. The competition has also pushed down prices on the main carriers, so don't exclude them when looking for a deal. ◈ www.tigerairways.com; www.jetstar.com; www.airasia.com

5 Changi International Airport
The opening of Terminal 3 in 2008 consolidated Changi's reputation as one of the world's best airports. Many people check in early to relax and use the facilities. The terminals are clean and efficient, and the Visitors Centre helps with information and reservations. ◈ Map V2 • 6542-1122 • www.changiairport.com

6 Traveling By Rail
Two rail options exist between Malaysia and Singapore. Each operates from Tanjong Pagar station. The daily service to Johor Bahru and Kuala Lumpur is operated by Malaysia's Keretapi Tanah Melayu (KTMB). It is slow but comfortable and reliable. The opulent Oriental Express makes a weekly passage between Bangkok and Singapore, stopping at Penang and Kuala Lumpur. ◈ KTMB: 6222-5165 • www.ktmb.com.my • Orient Express: 6392-3500 • www.orient-express.com

7 Traveling by Bus
Make the short hop to Malaysia's Johor Bahru using SBS bus 170 from Queen Street or SMRT 950 from Woodlands Interchange next to Woodlands MRT (www.plusliner.com & see p106). Passengers leave the bus at the checkpoint, so keep your ticket to board the next bus.

8 Traveling by Taxi
Licensed taxis to Malaysia are available at a Queen Street stand or by calling 6293-5546. These only travel to the checkpoint, where you must transfer to a Malaysian-registered cab.

9 By Private Car
Cars entering Singapore require an Autopass and Vehicle Entry Certificate from the immigration booths. Cars rented in Singapore need additional insurance to be driven in Malaysia and at least three-fourths of a tank of fuel before leaving. Driving is on the left in both countries.

10 By Ferry
Ferries are the best way to reach islands near Singapore. Catch ferries to Kusu and St. John's at Marina South Pier or rent boats to the Sisters' Islands and Pulau Hantu. The Indonesian islands of Batam and Bintan are reached from the Tanah Merah ferry terminal or Singapore Cruise Centre.

Left **An MRT train** Center **EZ link card** Right **Local transit bus**

Getting Around

1 Transportation from Changi

The easiest way to get to the city from Changi Airport is by the Mass Rapid Transit (MRT), taxi, or the airport shuttle bus, which stops at larger hotels. For two or more people, a taxi is the fastest, most economical way to get around. There are taxi stands at each of the terminals.

2 MRT

The efficient and cheap Mass Rapid Transit (MRT) network operates three lines across the island that run from 6am to midnight. The North-South Line runs from Jurong East to Marina Bay, the East-West Line shuttles from Pasir Ris and Changi Airport to Boon Lay, and the North-East Line operates from Punggol to HarbourFront.

3 Taxis

Taxis are normally inexpensive, although a complex system of peak hour and other surcharges can increase fares significantly. Rainstorms and rush hours are best avoided. Within the city center, wait at a taxi stand for a cab or call one of the operators to reserve ahead (fees apply).

4 EZ Link Cards

These pre-paid and refundable cards are an excellent way to use Singapore's extensive public transportation system. Available at any MRT station, they can be used on the MRT, LRT (overground light railway) and buses. One-, two-, or three-day Singapore Tourist Passes are also available from Changi Airport and MRT stations, or from www. singaporetouristpass.com

5 Buses

Singapore has a comprehensive network of buses. Fares vary according to distance and whether the bus is air-conditioned. Routes are more complicated to understand than the MRT for short-term visitors, so the transitlink online journey planner is useful.

6 SIA Hop-on Bus

This air-conditioned bus plies between more than 20 spots, including Chinatown, Orchard Road, Little India, and Sentosa. The usual fare of S$12 a day is reduced to S$3 for passengers travelling with Silk Air or Singapore Airlines.

7 Walking

Plan your walking routes carefully, because Singapore's heat and humidity can make even a short stroll exhausting. Take plenty of breaks to rest and rehydrate.

8 Car Rentals

Several major car rental companies operate in Singapore and the rental process is simple for holders of an international driving permit or an English-language license. Local driving behavior, such as tailgating and frequent lane changes, can be stressful, though.

9 Chauffeur Rental

Chauffeur-driven cars and mini-buses can be arranged by many hotels, at Changi Airport, or by rental firms. Depending on itinerary and group size, costs can be surprisingly reasonable.

10 Biking

Renting a bicycle is an ideal, if energetic, way to enjoy the straight, level paths of the East Coast Park, or the challenging Bukit Timah or Pulau Ubin nature reserves (see pp42–3). On the roads, however, a bike is an uncomfortable and unsafe way for visitors to travel.

Transport

Taxis
• Comfort Citicab: 6552-1111
• Premier/Silvercab: 6363-6888

Buses
• www.transitlink. com.sg
• www.siahopon. asiaone.com.sg

Car rentals
• www.avis.com.sg
• www.hertz.com

Left **Local Newspapers** Center **Visitor Information Center at Changi Airport** Right **A Map**

Sources of Information

1 Singapore Tourism Board

Visitors are well served by the efficient Singapore Tourism Board, which has offices in several countries abroad, and useful resources. There is a toll-free number for use in Singapore.
🕾 1800-736-2000

2 Websites

The Singapore Tourism Board's website, www.visitsingapore.com, is packed with information and suggested itineraries in various languages. Links to useful websites, such as www.hungrygowhere.com and www.ieatishootipost.blogspot.com, offer restaurant reviews.

3 Visitor Information Centers (VIC)

There are several visitor information centers in Singapore, including those at Changi Airport terminals 1, 2, and 3, and four branches in Central Singapore. Well-trained staff at all centers offer useful information and tips. 🕾 Orchard Rd. VIC: Map C5 • Orchard Rd./ Cairnhill Rd. 🕾 Valley Rd. VIC: Map A6 • 177 River Valley Rd. 🕾 Clarke Quay VIC: Map L3 • Clarke Quay MRT 🕾 Little India VIC: Map F4 • 73 Dunlop St., Inncrowd Backpackers Hostel • Touristline: 1800-736-2000 (toll-free in Singapore), (65) 6736-2000 (overseas)

4 Local Newspapers

The national daily broadsheet is the Straits Times, carrying world news from an Asian perspective. To glimpse the daily life of ordinary Singaporeans, the letters pages of free tabloids, Today and My Paper, can make interesting reading.

5 Local Magazines

Time Out Singapore is published every two weeks. Available at news stands, bookstores, and big supermarkets, it has good listings of current events all over the island, with an emphasis on the arts and music. Upcoming events are also detailed in the Singapore Tourism Board's monthly newsletter, which is available from visitor centers.

6 TV and Radio

Singapore has two local TV channels in English. Channel News Asia offers CNN-style rolling news, while Channel 5 shows drama and lifestyle imports from the US. On the radio, most local English-language channels play mainly western pop music. Hotels offer cable via StarHub, which covers international channels such as Star World, CNBC Live, HBO, and Discovery.

7 Maps

Visitor Information Centers and hotels provide free maps of the city center. These can also be picked up at hotels and tourist spots. The city is easy to navigate, so cumbersome street directories are rarely necessary.

8 Disabled Visitors

Although Singapore is working toward better accessibility for visitors with disabilities, wheelchair users may be frustrated by the lack of ramps in many places. MRT stations are equipped with elevators and many have braille and tactile flooring. Wheelchair-friendly taxis can be booked from the main taxi operators.

9 Gay and Lesbian Visitors

Homosexuality remains technically illegal in Singapore, despite a 2008 attempt to repeal the laws. However, these are rarely enforced and Singapore has a growing, but relatively discreet, gay scene. There are many gay bars near Tanjong Pagar Road.

10 Media Censorship

The Government of Singapore considers the local media a responsible partner in nation-building. The Singapore press has responded to this policy with effective self-censorship. There is little overtly political activity and rarely are foreigners visiting or living here politically active.

Streetsmart

Left **Cheap eats in hawker centers** Center **Bukit Timah Nature Reserve** Right **Chinese souvenirs**

🔟 Budget Tips

Budget Airlines
Various budget airlines ply the region. Visitors arriving from within Asia or those planning to travel around the region will do well to check for discounted fares from airlines such as Tiger Airways (with routes throughout Asia), Cebu Pacific (to the Philippines), Bangkok Airways (to Koh Samui, Thailand), and JetStar (throughout Southeast Asia and to India).
❧ www.tigerairways.com; www.cebupacificair.com; www.bangkokair.com; www.jetstar.com

Getting Around
Passengers flying Singapore Airlines can enjoy discounted tickets on the SIA Hop-on Bus, which stops at over 20 favorite tourist spots. The bus and MRT systems sell Singapore Tourist Pass one-price tickets for unlimited rides all day. They cost S$18 a day *(see p106)*. ❧ www.singaporeair.com; www.thesingaporetouristpass.com

Cheap Eats
Singapore's hawker centers and food courts offer a truly wide variety of fine local and international dishes. An entire meal with a drink can cost as little as S$5. At hawker centers outside the city center, the same dishes can be found for as little as S$3.

Cheap Nights Out
Most pubs and bars have daily happy hours, from afternoon to early evening, depending on the place. Discounts can include cheap jugs of beer or two-for-one drinks, but premium liquor is rarely included. Some nightclubs have Ladies' Nights when they offer free drinks to women all night long.

Free Parks and Gardens
As well as offering free admission to most of its parks and gardens, the National Parks Board offers free guided walks on select weekends at parks such as Fort Canning Park and Bukit Timah Nature Reserve.
❧ www.nparks.gov.sg

Free Entry to Museums
Museums run by the National Heritage Board, such as the National Museum of Singapore and the Asian Civilisations Museum, have free admission every Friday evening (7–9pm) and on some public holidays.
❧ www.nhb.gov.sg

Free Cultural Events
Besides hosting free religious and cultural festivals, the city holds free arts performances, including street buskers, live music, museum talks, movie screenings, and fringe events for festivals and exhibitions.
❧ www.visitsingapore.com

Discount Tours
Hippo Tours sells Singapore Sightseeing Passes. The 1- and 2-day passes offer unlimited rides on the open-top Hippo tour bus, which stops at many major attractions around the city. There are five optional themed city tours. The bus is very good value for money; it is the cheapest tour option in the city.
❧ www.ducktours.com.sg

Cheap Stays
Although more expensive than their Southeast Asian counterparts, budget hotels and hostels in Singapore offer excellent safety for guests and are packed with convenient services such as travel libraries, public lounges, Internet, telephone services, and laundry.

Good Buys
The 24-hour Mustafa Centre *(see p76)* is the cheapest place to buy souvenirs, t-shirts, knick-knacks, Singapore Airlines hostess costumes, and more. The price here is fixed and usually much lower than at stores in the center of town. For some really serious shopping, visit during the Great Singapore Sale, every June through July.

Left **Kiosk selling phone cards** Center **An ATM** Right **Woman using a computer at an Internet café**

🔟 Banking and Communications

1 Banks, ATMs, and Credit Cards

Most major international banks have branches in Singapore, with local banking hours between 10am–3pm Monday–Friday and 9:30am–1pm Saturday. ATMs that accept cards linked to Cirrus or PLUS networks can be found in shopping malls and MRT stations. Visa, American Express, JCB, Diners Club, and MasterCard are widely accepted but smaller retailers may charge extra for credit card purchases.

2 Changing Money and Transferring Funds

Currency can be changed at any hotel or bank, but best rates are given by licensed money-changers operating from booths in shopping centers and commercial hubs. Wire transfer by Western Union can be arranged at any SingPost outlet.
🔗 www.singpost.com

3 GST Refund

The 5 percent Goods & Services Tax levied on all purchases can be reclaimed by visitors spending at least S$100 a day at a store that participates in the GST Refund scheme. Upon purchase, ask for a GST Refund form. Fill in the form and present it with your receipt and the goods purchased to the customs officer at your

point of departure. You will be given a voucher to present at a kiosk where the refund can be given on the spot, credited to your card, or transferred to a bank account.
🔗 www.customs.gov.sg

4 Mail

SingPost provides efficient mail and package handling from many locations including Ngee Ann City and Lucky Plaza, both on Orchard Road, and Suntec City. Hours vary between outlets. Overseas post-cards cost 50 cents each and letters S$1.10 each. Poste Restante services are at SingPost's Eunos Branch, a bit far from the city center.

5 Public Telephones

Find coin- and card-operated phones in shopping malls and MRT stations. Local calls cost 10 cents for three minutes. Most phones accept payment by credit card or pre-paid phone cards. These can be purchased from SingPost outlets or 7-Eleven shops that also sell international pre-paid phone cards.

6 Calling Singapore

Singapore's country code is 65. There are no area codes within Singapore. Local phone numbers are eight digits and begin with 6. Cell phone lines also have eight-digit numbers, but begin with an 8 or a 9.

7 Cell Phones

Singapore operates on two cell phone networks, GSM900 and GSM1800. There are three local cell phone service providers – SingTel, M1, and StarHub.

8 Internet Access

All major international hotels provide in-room Internet access, and many have wireless Internet access through-out. There are usually Wifi hotspots in the city's cafés, and many Internet cafés are located in central shopping areas.

9 Business Centers

Most big hotels have well-equipped business centers, some operating round the clock. Smaller and budget hotels are also able to offer fax, copy, and other services from their front offices.

10 Public Holidays

Singapore has 10 public holidays. These include: New Year's Day (Jan 1), Chinese New Year (held over two days, Jan/Feb), Good Friday (Mar/Apr), Labour Day (May 1), Vesak Day (usually May), National Day (Aug 9), Deepavali (usually Oct/Nov), Hari Raya Haji (in Nov), and Christmas (Dec 25). However, many religious holidays have no set date, but fall according to the lunar calendar or other calculation.

Left **City policeman** Center **Pharmacy sign** Right **Bottled water**

Security and Health

1 Emergency Numbers
Emergency numbers in Singapore can be dialed free from public phones. Dial 999 for police, 995 for ambulance and fire emergencies.

2 Police
Singapore is generally a very safe city. Laws are strictly enforced by an efficient police force. Many minor offenses carry a fine and a foreigner accused of breaking the law may not necessarily have access to legal advice from his home consulate.

3 Theft Prevention
Despite a very low crime rate, pickpocketing does occur, especially in crowded areas such as the night markets in Bugis Street and Chinatown. Most hotels have in-room safes, or important items can be placed within the hotel's main safe. It is a good idea to keep passports, airline tickets, and credit cards in here – a photocopy of your passport is acceptable as identification.

4 Hospitals
Singapore's standard of health care is known to be one of the best in the world. The most central hospitals in the city are Mount Elizabeth Hospital, Gleneagles Hospital, and Singapore General Hospital.

5 Infectious Diseases
In recent years diseases such as Severe Acute Respiratory Syndrome (SARS) and Avian Influenza have made headlines. In 2003, Singapore's efficient response to SARS earned kudos. Government agencies control imports of poultry infected with the Bird Flu virus.

6 Mosquito-borne Illnesses
Singapore has been malaria-free for decades, but other mosquito-borne illnesses pose a problem, such as dengue and chikungunya. Mosquito repellent is advisable.

7 Pharmacies
There are branches of Guardian and Watsons in most shopping malls around the city. Remember prescriptions from overseas doctors are not accepted.
⊗ www.guardian.com.sg; www.watsons.com.sg

8 Drinking Water and Food Safety
Tap water is safe to drink. Bottled water is available at convenience stores, cafés, and restaurants. Street food is generally safe. Hygiene standards are rated by the government, and restaurants and food stalls failing basic health requirements are strictly closed down. The highest rating is "A".

9 Women Travelers
Singapore sees many solo female business travelers. The crime rate against women is low.

10 Consulates
It is recommended that you register your travel dates with your embassy or consulate, to ease assistance in case you run into problems.

Embassies

US Embassy:
• Map S3; 27 Napier Rd; 6476-9100

British High Commission:
• Map S3; 100 Tanglin Rd; 6473-9333

Australian High Commission:
• Map S3; 25 Napier Rd; 6836-4100

Canadian High Commission:
• Map L3; One George St. #11-01; 6854-5900

Emergency and Hospital Numbers

• **Police:** 999

• **Fire/Ambulance:** 995

• **Gleneagles Hospital:** Map S3; Napier Rd; 6473-7222

• **Mount Elizabeth Hospital:** Map B4, C4; near Orchard Rd; 6731-2218

• **Singapore General Hospital:** Map J5; Outram Rd; 6321-4111

Left **Bicycle trishaw rides** Right **DUCKtours**

≊10 Organized Tours

1 Trishaw Tours

Bicycle trishaw rides through the city's main tourist neighborhoods let you relax and see the sights at a leisurely pace. ✎ *Singapore Explorer, Chinatown Trishaw Park • 6339-6833 • Open 10am–10pm daily • www.singaporeexplorer.com.sg*

2 Singapore Walks

Themed walking tours through ethnic neighborhoods are conducted by expert guides who give details about major attractions, local customs, history, and heritage. Different walks are scheduled on different days (except Sundays and public holidays). No reservations are required – just show up and pay the tour guide. ✎ *www.singaporewalks.com*

3 Singapore River Tours

A few companies conduct tours of the Singapore River in old-style "bumboats," similar to boats that would load and unload ships docked in the bay. Trips cruise past Robertson Quay, Clarke Quay, and Boat Quay out into Marina Bay for views of the city skyline. Commentary is via a pre-recorded tape. The boats can be boarded at Merlion Park, Raffles Landing Site, and other stops along the way. ✎ *6336-6111 • www.rivercruise.com.sg*

4 DUCKtours

This unusual amphibious craft provides a city tour with a twist. It goes from land into the sea and back onto land again, combining both a bus and boat tour. ✎ *Suntec Galleria • 6338-6877 • Open 9am–6:30pm daily • www.ducktours.com.sg*

5 Peranakan Tour

Times World runs a tour to Katong, a neighborhood in Singapore's East Coast that was popular with the Peranakan community in the early 1900s. The tour introduces Peranakan architecture, costume, and cuisine, with some shopping and food-tasting included in the itinerary. A minimum of six passengers is required to run the tour. ✎ *Times World, 545 Orchard Rd. • 6738-5505 • www.timesworld.com.sg*

6 Paranormal Tours

Local ghostbusters, Singapore Paranormal Investigators, conduct two tours designed to be as creepy as possible through Singapore's allegedly most haunted areas. Not recommended for young children. ✎ *www.spi.com.sg*

7 Heartlands Tour

Tour East takes visitors to East Coast and Changi, suburban satellite towns built around government housing clusters. It provides an interesting glimpse into the lives of Singaporeans. ✎ *Tour East, 15 Cairnhill Rd. • 6738-2622 • www.singaporetours.com.sg*

8 World War II Site Tours

Hello Singapore organizes half-day tours to the island's World War II battlegrounds, surrender sites, and POW camps. ✎ *Hello Singapore, 100 Orchard Rd., Meridien Shopping Centre #02–17/18 • 6732-4188 • www.luxury.com.sg*

9 Chinese Junk Cruises

Water Tours offer cruises in a replica of an old Chinese junk. This large ship is similar to the type used in the days of Admiral Zheng He, or Cheng Ho, the 15th-century commander of the most famous Chinese fleet. Four daily tours include breakfast, lunch, tea, or dinner. ✎ *Water Tours, 1 Maritime Square, Harbourfront Centre • 6533-9811 • www.watertours.com.sg*

10 Spice Tour

At-sunrice offers a unique tour of a spice garden, including a demonstration of how to make an Asian curry paste, followed by a hands-on cooking class. ✎ *At-sunrice, Fort Canning Park, Fort Canning Centre • 6336-9353 • www.at-sunrice.com*

Left **A rainy day in Singapore** Center **Public warning signs** Right **Lining up for a taxi**

🔟 Things to Avoid

1 Overheating
To really get the most out of your time in Singapore, it pays to slow down. Opt to dress in cool, casual clothes. The heat and humidity here tend to drain you of energy fast.

2 Dehydration
Constant perspiration leaves you at a risk of dehydration. Bottled water is available at convenience stores, food courts, and cafés across town. It is a good idea to carry water with you everywhere you go.

3 Exposure
In the tropics, downpours can come with very little forewarning. Always carry an umbrella with you, as most locals do. Singaporeans use them as parasols, especially the compact umbrellas that are covered in reflective silver fabric. They can help prevent sunburn and keep you cool.

4 Freezing
The air conditioning in malls, office buildings, and movie theaters is usually kept at very low temperatures so it is a good idea to carry a jacket, a wrap, or a long-sleeved shirt.

5 Peak-hour Taxis
Public transportation is generally reliable and cheap. However, try to find a taxi just after office hours or during a rainstorm and you may find yourself in a line for up to 40 minutes. There is often a rush for taxis just before midnight, since a 50 percent surcharge is added to all fares between midnight and 6am. Taxis can be reserved when you need them, but they may take a long time to arrive. It is therefore a good idea to find out the locations of the nearest MRT stations and major bus routes that serve your hotel.

6 Driving
While Avis and Hertz do rent cars, it is not recommended for visitors to drive themselves. Electronic Road Pricing charges and parking require pre-paid cash cards and tickets. Traffic can be frustrating, and so can the behavior of some local drivers, who change lanes frequently. Parking can be hard to find, too. The city's public transportation is efficient, cheap, and reliable, and is therefore a good option.

7 Touts
Touts are illegal in Singapore, but you will still come across them in certain shopping malls along Orchard Road and elsewhere. Beware of aggressive sales tactics. It is always wise to check on the international warranties for relevant purchases, too. The Singapore Tourism Board *(see p107)* also operates a system to alert the public and visitors to the country of disreputable retailers.

8 Smoking
It is illegal to smoke indoors, even in restaurants and pubs. Some alfresco pubs and cafés have small sections where smoking is allowed. Visitors must remember that smoking is also forbidden in taxi lines, and any other lines of more than five people. If caught smoking, the maximum fine is S$1000.

9 Drugs
Singapore's drug policy is very strict – import, possession, and use of illegal narcotics all carry a penalty. This may even include the death sentence if the quantities involved are large enough for a trafficking verdict or if the authorities can prove an intent to traffic. These laws apply to foreigners as well.

10 Crowds
On weekends, shopping malls and attractions become crowded with local families, foreign maids, and workers all enjoying their day off. Places like Orchard Road and Little India become especially crowded, so if you are heading out on the weekend, be prepared to encounter crowds and lines everywhere.

Left **A hotel reception** Center **Keep small change for tips** Right **Drinks at a bar**

🔟 Accommodation and Dining Tips

1 Hotel Reservations

Singapore's hotels enjoy super-high occupancy rates year-round, so it is highly recommended to reserve early. If you do arrive without having a reservation, the Singapore Hotel Association operates Hotel Reservations counters at all Changi Airport arrival halls round the clock, seven days a week (see p105).
⬥ Singapore Hotel Association, 260 Tanjong Pagar Rd., #04–01/03 • 6513-0233 • www. sha.org.sg

2 Rack Rates

Hotels charge a standard room rate that includes breakfast, newspaper delivery, and some other added benefits. Several international hotels now charge a "best rate", depending on the dates of your stay and the time that you book. In some hotels, discounted prices are available for guests who do not need any additional services.

3 Peak Season

Because Singapore hosts business events and conventions year-round, there is no strictly defined peak season. During the summer months of July and August, vacationers tend to replace business travelers. The busiest season for hotels, however, is from

Christmas through Chinese New Year when top rates apply.

4 Long-stay

Hotels offer discounted long-stay rates, but a number of operators have serviced apartments at varying degrees of luxury for long-term guests. These generally have kitchens furnished with cooking utensils and other domestic conveniences. Long-stay apartments can be a good option for families.

5 Hotel Taxes and Tipping

Hotels will sometimes quote "plus, plus" or ++ following their rates. This means you will be charged the rate plus an additional 10 percent service charge and 7 percent Goods and Services Tax (GST). Tipping is not expected in hotels. However, it is not uncommon for travelers to tip the bellhops in hotels from S$2–5 per bag.

6 Restaurant Reservations

Inexpensive restaurants seldom accept reservations. For some upmarket restaurants, a reservation is highly recommended.

7 Meal Times

Most restaurants close between mealtimes to set up for the next seating. If you find

yourself hungry in the mid-morning, afternoon, or late at night, it is best to try your hotel coffee-shop, a café, a hawker center, or a food court. Many Western fast-food chains have franchises in Singapore as well.

8 Restaurant Taxes and Tipping

Almost all restaurant and bar bills will include a 10 percent service charge and 7 percent GST. Tipping is not practiced in Singapore, but many diners leave small change behind for the server. This is not considered impolite. Tips added onto a credit card slip will probably not be given to the server.

9 Dress Codes

The term "dress casual" means no shorts, flip-flops, or tank tops. Most occasions requiring special attire request guests to "dress casual." Women should wear a dress, pants, or a skirt with a blouse and men should wear pants and collared shirts.

10 Wine and Spirits

The legal drinking age in Singapore is 18. Duty-free concessions allow each visitor to bring 1 liter of spirits, 1 liter of wine or port, and 1 liter of beer. Alcohol is taxed heavily in Singapore – drinks in restaurants and bars tend to be on the pricey side.

Left **Shangri-La Hotel pool** Center **Goodwood Park Hotel** Right **A suite at Raffles Hotel**

Super Luxury Hotels

1 The St. Regis Singapore
The exclusive St. Regis is famous for its superb butler service. The truly luxurious guest rooms have hand-painted wall coverings, designer upholstery, special bed linen, and French marble bathrooms. Facilities include a fitness center, spa, and rooftop pool. ✪ Map S3 • 29 Tanglin Rd. • 6506-6888 • www. starwoodhotels.com/stregis • $$$$$

2 The Ritz-Carlton, Millenia Singapore
This hotel has top-quality service standards. Located near convention facilities and the Central Business District, it is typically booked by high-profile business guests. Contemporary art pieces grace public areas and rooms. Marble bathrooms have huge tubs. ✪ Map P2 • 7 Raffles Avenue • 6337-8888 • www.ritzcarlton.com • $$$$$

3 Shangri-La Hotel
With sprawling gardens, the Shangri-La is an oasis in the city. Guests can choose from three styles of accommodation: the classically elegant rooms of the Valley Wing, the urban resort feel of the Garden Wing, or contemporary rooms in the Tower Wing. ✪ Map A3 • 22 Orange Grove Rd. • 6737-3644 • www.shangri-la.com • $$$$

4 Four Seasons Hotel
This 20-story building is just a jog away from the Botanic Gardens. Rooms are smaller than average, but have charming continental decor and highly comfortable beds. The restaurant One-Ninety does a great Sunday brunch. ✪ Map A4 • 190 Orchard Boulevard • 6734-1110 • www. fourseasons.com • $$$$$

5 Raffles Hotel
Raffles is pure romance and nostalgia, with rooms restored to resemble the hotel's 1930s heyday. Award-winning dining options and a central location add to its appeal. ✪ Map M1, N1 • 1 Beach Rd. • 6337-1886 • www.singapore. raffles.com • $$$$$

6 Mandarin Oriental
The slick and polished Mandarin has a glossy black marble lobby and classic Asian art and furnishings. It is close to conference venues and the Central Business District. ✪ Map N2 • 5 Raffles Avenue • 6338-0066 • www.mandarin oriental.com • $$$$$

7 The Fullerton Hotel
Converted from the former General Post Office, this gracious landmark has guest rooms with high ceilings and long windows. Its state-of-the-art telecommunications facilities and workspaces are perfect for business guests. ✪ Map M3 • 1 Fullerton Square • 6733-8388 • www.fullertonhotel. com • $$$$$

8 Amara Sanctuary Resort, Sentosa
Built from a 1930s-era military barrack, the Amara combines tropical colonial architecture with contemporary resort-style interiors. The spa is to die for, and there is a rooftop pool with sea views. ✪ Map S3 • 1 Larkhill Rd., Sentosa • 6825-3888 • www. amarasanctuary.com • $$$

9 Fairmont Hotel
Raffles Hotel's sister property, the Fairmont has contemporary rooms. The bathrooms feature innovations such as rain forest showerheads and glass countertops. The hotel also has the largest spa in town (see p54). ✪ Map M1, M2 • 80 Bras Basah Rd. • 6339-7777 • www.fairmont.com • $$$$

10 Goodwood Park Hotel
Converted from the 1900s Teutonia Club for German expatriates, Goodwood's oldest wing is a national monument. Rooms vary in decor from colonial to resort-style. The dining options are excellent. ✪ Map B3 • 22 Scotts Rd. • 6737-7411 • www.goodwood parkhotel. com • $$$

Note: Unless otherwise stated, all hotels accept credit cards, and have en-suite bathrooms and air conditioning.

Price Categories

For a standard, double room per night (with breakfast, if included), taxes, and extra charges.

$	under S$100
$$	S$100–200
$$$	S$200–300
$$$$	S$300–400
$$$$$	over S$400

The pool at the Singapore Marriott Hotel

🔟 Business Hotels

1 Singapore Marriott Hotel

Housed in a landmark pagoda-shaped tower, the Marriott offers good city views in every direction. Rooms have luxurious bedding, large desks and good communications facilities. The hotel also has an excellent café and two popular nightclubs.
⬡ Map B4 • 320 Orchard Rd. • 6735-5800 • www. marriot.com • $$$$$

2 Grand Hyatt

The check-in area here is located out of view of the main doors. While the Grand Rooms are larger, the Terrace Wing rooms have bright workspaces with Internet and entertainment options. ⬡ Map B4 • 10 Scotts Rd. • 6738-1234 • www.singapore.grand. hyatt.com • $$$$$

3 Sheraton Towers

Situated at the edge of the Central Business District, the Sheraton is popular for social and business receptions. The staff are professional, especially the butler service. The Cabana rooms face the rooftop pool. Suites have creative themes. ⬡ Map C2 • 39 Scotts Rd. • 6737-6888 • www.sheraton singapore. com • $$$$

4 Pan Pacific

The largest hotel in Singapore, Pan Pacific's business center occupies a floor with private offices, meeting rooms, and a lounge supported by plenty of secretarial staff. Its award-winning restaurants serve North Indian, Japanese, and Cantonese cuisine.
⬡ Map N2 • 7 Raffles Boulevard • 6336-8111 • www.panpacific.com • $$$$

5 InterContinental

Built atop a cluster of pre-war shophouses, the hotel has absorbed these original structures as well as local style into its decor. While not directly in the city center, it is located above an MRT station not far from the Suntec Convention Center. ⬡ Map G5 • 80 Middle Rd. • 6338-7600 • www.singapore. intercontinental.com • $$$$

6 M Hotel

One of the few international business class hotels located inside the Shenton Way financial district, M Hotel caters to business travelers, emphasizing convenience for working guests. Weekend guests can enjoy good discounts.
⬡ Map K6 • 81 Anson Rd. • 6224-1133 • www. m-hotel.com • $$$

7 Crowne Plaza Changi Airport Hotel

This is Singapore's first international business hotel to be located at the airport, which is still close enough to make quick trips into town. It is also near the Singapore Expo as well as the East Coast industrial parks supported by Changi Airport. ⬡ Map V2 • 75 Airport Boulevard • 6823-5300 • www. crowneplaza.com • $$$$

8 Marina Mandarin

Built around an airy atrium lobby, this business hotel is connected to the Marina Square shopping mall. The views from the rooms that face the bay are terrific. ⬡ Map N2 • 6 Raffles Boulevard • 6845-1000 • www.marina-mandarin.com.sg • $$$

9 Conrad Centennial

The Conrad is ideally situated for business travelers. Its guest rooms are located in two towers and feature state-of-the-art communications facilities. They are supported by conference rooms and a business center. ⬡ Map N2 • 2 Temasek Boulevard • 6334-8888 • www. conradhotels.com • $$$$$

10 Hilton Singapore Hotel

The Hilton is a landmark on Orchard Road and is just a short walk from the city's best shopping malls. Rooms facing the road have views of the Thai Embassy gardens.
⬡ Map A4 • 581 Orchard Rd. • 6737-2233 • www. singapore.hilton.com • $$$$

Left **Sentosa Resort and Spa** Center **YMCA International House** Right **Orchard Parade Hotel**

TOP 10 Family Hotels

1 Rasa Sentosa Resort
Sentosa's only beachfront hotel is an attractive choice for families. There's plenty to keep children occupied, including a pool and play area, as well as the aquarium next door. All rooms have a private balcony overlooking Fort Siloso or Singapore harbor. ✆ Map S3 • 101 Siloso Rd. • 6235-1666 • www.shangri-la.com • $$$$

2 Siloso Beach Resort
The glass walls of this resort offer great views of the beach, and it is just a short walk to the sea. There are one- and two-bedroom villas, as well as the rooms in the main hotel. The leisure facilities are excellent, and there is a waterfall pool. ✆ Map S3 • 51 Imbiah Walk, Sentosa • 6722-3333 • www.silosobeachresort.com • $$$

3 Sentosa Resort and Spa
Home to the award-winning Spa Botanica, this luxurious resort is set amid lush greenery and tropical fishponds. Ideal both for couples and families, all of its rooms boast plasma TVs and most promise a garden view. The Cliff restaurant has superb seafood. ✆ Map S3 • 2 Bukit Manis Rd. • 6275-0331 • www.thesentosa.com • $$$$

4 Treasure Resort, Sentosa
Rooms at the Treasure Resort, once the old British Barracks, have a colonial feel, with high ceilings and a balcony or deck area. This resort is situated next to Imbiah station, so transportation to the mainland is easy using the Sentosa Express (see pp26–7). ✆ Map S3 • 23 Beach View • 6271-2002 • www.treasure-resort.com • $$$

5 YMCA International House
Of the several YMCAs in Singapore it's hard to beat International House for location, just a couple of minutes' walk from the National Museum and other historic sights as well as Orchard Road. It also has a cafe, pool, and a gym. The rooms range from four-bed dorms to family suites. ✆ Map E6 • 1 Orchard Rd. • 6235-2498 • www.ymcaih.com.sg • $$$

6 YWCA Fort Canning Lodge
The YWCA shares its great location with the YMCA. The well-equipped rooms and family suites are a good size with views of the pool and park. There is a tennis court and self-service laundry, and the staff are friendly and helpful. ✆ Map E6 • 6 Fort Canning Rd. • 6338-4222 • www.ywcafclodge.org.sg • $$$

7 Parkroyal
Close to Arab Street, the Parkroyal has good facilities at a reasonable price. Rooms are slightly bland but clean. Inter-connecting rooms are available, too. The huge rooftop pool is popular with children. ✆ Map H5 • 7500 Beach Rd. • 6505-5666 • www.parkroyalhotels.com • $$$

8 Orchard Parade Hotel
This is a great location at a good price. The hotel has a pool, laundry facilities, and family studios with lounge and dining areas. ✆ Map A4 • 1 Tanglin Rd. • 6737-1133 • www.orchardparade.com.sg • $$$

9 Fraser Place
For stays of more than a week, Fraser Place has well-equipped one-, two-, and three-bedroom apartments on the waterfront. There is a playground and a pool with a supermarket and cafés nearby. ✆ Map J2 • 11 Unity St. • 6736-4800 • www.frasershospitality.com • $$$

10 Fraser Suites
Like its sister property, this long-stay hotel offers luxurious one-, two-, and three-bedroom apartments with kitchens and a playground. ✆ Map S3 • 491A River Valley Rd. • www.frasershospitality.com • $$$$$

Unless otherwise stated, all hotels accept credit cards, and have en-suite bathrooms and air conditioning.

Price Categories

For a standard, double room per night (with breakfast if included), taxes, and extra charges.	
$	under S$100
$$	S$100–200
$$$	S$200–300
$$$$	S$300–400
$$$$$	over S$400

Left **Swimming pools at the Holiday Inn Park View**

Value-for-Money Hotels

1 Hotel Bencoolen
Only a few minutes' walk away from Orchard Road and Little India, the Bencoolen's location makes it a good choice. The rooms are clean and equipped with TV and coffee-making facilities. Breakfast is a western-style buffet and there is a modest rooftop pool.
🏵 Map F5 • 47 Bencoolen St. • 6336-0822 • www. hotelbencoolen.com • $$$

2 Hotel Grand Central
Nowhere else in the city will you get such a great location for the price. Do not expect much in the way of facilities, but it may appeal to visitors who use a hotel as a crash pad and want to be close to Orchard Road.
🏵 Map D5 • 22 Cavenagh Rd. • 6737-9944 • www. grandcentral.com.sg • $$

3 RELC International Hotel
RELC offers a good combination of location and facilities at a very good price. There's a decent range of rooms and prices, but all are reasonably large and equipped with balconies, cable TV, fridge, and coffee-making facilities. The free breakfast is not too great, but you will find tempting options on Orchard Road just 10 minutes' walk away.
🏵 Map A2 • 30 Orange Grove Rd. • 6885-7888 • www.relcih.com.sg • $$

4 Robertson Quay Hotel
The same great location as the Fraser Suites, but at a lower price. The rooms and bathrooms are very small and basic. The best and quietest rooms face the river. There's a small pool on the roof and an outside bar. The restaurants and bars of Robertson Quay are moments away.
🏵 Map J2 • 15 Merbau Rd. • 6735-3333 • www.robert sonquayhotel.com.sg • $$

5 Lloyd's Inn
More of a budget motel than a hotel, Lloyd's is simple with no pool and not many facilities. But the location is excellent and sur-prisingly quiet for one at Orchard Road. 🏵 Map D6 • 2 Lloyd Rd. • 6737-7309 • www.lloydinn.com • $$

6 Strand Hotel
The Strand does not look like a budget place. Rooms are large and colorful with a range of deluxe and family rooms, which can accommodate up to seven guests. "Special" rooms are vividly decorated.
🏵 Map F5 • 25 Bencoolen St. • 6338-1866 • www. strandhotel.com.sg • $$

7 The Inn at Temple Street
Right in the heart of the Chinatown Conservation Area, this award-winning inn takes up a row of five renovated shophouses. It is not strong on modern comforts and the rooms are small, but it has a charm that is unusual at this price. 🏵 Map K4 • 36 Temple St. • 6221-5333 • www.theinn.com.sg • $$

8 Peninsula Excelsior Hotel
The result of a merger of the Excelsior and Peninsula hotels gives you twice the facilities and two pools. Ask for a room facing Marina Bay – you will not get a better view at the price. 🏵 Map L2 • 5 Coleman St. • 6337-8080 • www.ytchotels.com. sg • $$$

9 Holiday Inn Park View
Though not absolutely budget, this hotel has rooms that are large, clean, and equipped with fridges and coffee-making facilities. There is a decent breakfast buffet, service standards are high, and there are pools for adults and children.
🏵 Map C4 • 11 Cavenagh Rd. • 6733-8333 • www. holidayinn.com • $$$

10 Summer View Hotel
This inexpensive hotel is surrounded by a host of attractions. It has all the basics – breakfast buffet in its Thai restaurant, cable TV, Internet, and coffee-making facilities, but no pool. 🏵 Map F5 • 173 Bencoolen St. • 6338-1122 • www.summer viewhotel.com.sg • $$$

Left **Berjaya Hotel's restaurant** Center **Room at Naumi Hotel** Right **Lobby at Scarlet Hotel**

TOP 10 Boutique Hotels

1 The Scarlet Hotel

An experience for the senses, every inch of the Scarlet is swathed in deep sumptuous velvet, silk, and satin, with bespoke furnishings and glistening lacquer accents. Suites are intimate. Standard and deluxe rooms are tiny. ⊗ Map K5 • 33 Erskine Rd. • 6511-3333 • www. thescarlethotel.com • $$$

2 New Majestic Hotel

An experiment in whimsical design, each room here is decorated by a local designer or artist, with site-specific artwork and contemporary furnishings. This is a fashionable address for cocktails and modern Chinese dining. ⊗ Map J5 • 31-37 Bukit Pasoh Rd. • 6511-4700 • www. newmajestichotel.com • $$$$

3 Link Hotel

This unique Art Deco property is the result of the government's first public housing project. Located in a charming old suburb not far from Chinatown, the hotel has interiors in contemporary teakwood with lively ethnic themes. ⊗ Map T3 • 50 Tiong Bahru Rd. • 6622-8585 • www.linkhotel. com.sg • $$$

4 Hotel 1929

Contemporary chic design is used to maximize space and

brighten up this little hotel in a renovated shophouse located in the heart of Chinatown. Rooms are small. Its restaurant, Ember, is award-winning. ⊗ Map J4 • 50 Keong Saik Rd. • 6347-1929 • www.hotel1929.com • $$$

5 Albert Court Hotel

This cozy little hotel is decorated with local Peranakan textiles, carved wood furnishings, and traditional floral tiles, to charming nostalgic effect. Facilities are limited, but the coffee shop has an excellent menu of local favorites. ⊗ Map F4 • 180 Albert St. • 6339-3939 • www. albertcourt.com.sg • $$

6 Gallery Hotel

Singapore's first hotel to sport contemporary artistic design uses bold colors and Post-Modern architecture to create eye-catching rooms. The cantilevered glass lap pool juts out over the street below. ⊗ Map J2 • 1 Nanson Rd. • 6849-8686 • www.galleryhotel. com.sg • $$

7 Naumi Hotel

This stylish property is part business hotel – with its central location and 24-hour butler service – and part boutique hotel, being smaller and more intimate than most. Rooms and facilities at the Naumi focus on

state-of-the-art technology and edgy design. ⊗ Map G6 • 41 Seah St. • 6403-6000 • www. naumihotel.com • $$$$

8 Berjaya Hotel

Tucked away in the picturesque backstreets of Chinatown, Berjaya is built from converted shophouses, which means it is big on charm but has few facilities. Rooms are small and decorated in European style. ⊗ Map K5 • 83 Duxton Rd. • 6227-7678 • www.berjaya hotels-resorts.com • $$$$

9 The Keong Saik Hotel

Another boutique hotel built from old shophouses, with small, sparsely furnished rooms. The hardwood floors are clean, and decorative molding surrounds windows overlooking an attractive Chinatown lane. ⊗ Map J4 • 69 Keong Saik Rd. • 6223-0660 • www. keongsaikhotel.com.sg • $$

10 The Royal Peacock Hotel

This property is located in an area known for heritage hotels, such as the Keong Saik. The Royal Peacock is similar, but its rooms have bold, dark tones. Reserve a room with a window, since not all have them. ⊗ Map J4 • 55 Keong Saik Rd. • 6223-3522 • www. royalpeacockhotel.com • $$

Note: Unless otherwise stated, all hotels accept credit cards, and have en-suite bathrooms and air conditioning.

Price Categories

For a standard, double room per night (with breakfast if included), taxes, and extra charges.

$	under S$100
$$	S$100–200
$$$	S$200–300
$$$$	S$300–400
$$$$$	over S$400

Left **The lounge at the InnCrowd Backpackers' Hostel**

🔟 Cheap Sleeps

1 Perak Hotel
The friendly front-desk staff make guests feel at home in this small guesthouse. Private rooms are very clean, with dressing tables, closets, and tiny en-suite bathrooms. A casual lobby café serves breakfast. ◎ Map F4 • 12 Perak Rd. • 6299-7733 • www.peraklodge.net • $$

2 Backpacker Cozy Corner Guest House
Single and double-bed rooms are small, simple, and very clean, but none have en-suite bathrooms. Dormitory rooms are available and facilities include Internet, laundry service, kitchenette, and sundeck. ◎ Map G5 • 490 North Bridge Rd. • 6339-6128 • www.cozycornerguest.com • $

3 hangout@mt.emily
Designed for image-conscious budget travelers, hangout has small, spartan, bright rooms with a funky feel and contemporary decor. Private rooms with en-suite are available. ◎ Map E4 • 10A Upper Wilkie Rd. • 6438-5588 • www.hangouthotels.com • $$

4 The Hive Backpackers' Hostel
Not quite centrally located, but clean and safe, this hostel has private rooms – some with en-suite bathrooms – and dorms, which are all air-conditioned. Breakfast is included and a lounge offers cable TV plus free Internet access. ◎ Map G2 • 624 Serangoon Rd. • 6341-5041 • www.thehivebackpackers.com • $

5 The InnCrowd Backpackers' Hostel
A very popular and well-planned place, this hostel is clean and spacious. The air-conditioned dorms and private rooms are supported by stylish bathrooms, a kitchenette, an inexpensive pub, Internet facilities, a travel library, and a rooftop sundeck. ◎ Map F4 • 73 Dunlop Street • 6296-9169 • www.the-inncrowd.com • $

6 Sleepy Sam's
With a nice relaxed location in Kampong Glam, this charming guesthouse is in a pretty traditional building that is surrounded by late-night cafés. Both private rooms and dorms are available here. A café, Internet-access, free breakfast, kitchenette, and lounge complete the facilities. ◎ Map H5 • 55 Bussorah St. • 9277-4988 • www.sleepysams.com • $

7 Summer Tavern
The location of this hostel is superb, within walking distance of Chinatown, Clarke Quay, Boat Quay, and the Colonial District. Dorms and private rooms with shared bath offer good security, and free Internet, breakfast, and lockers are available in the common areas. ◎ Map L3 • 31 Carpenter St. • 6535-6601 • www.summertavern.com • $

8 Bugis Backpackers
Though very basic, Bugis has conveniences such as a kitchenette, air-conditioned private rooms and dorms, and a launderette. ◎ Map G5 • 162B Rochor Rd. • 6338-5581 • www.bugisbackpackers.com • $

9 Fernloft Backpacker Hostel
A terrific Chinatown location adds to the appeal of this guesthouse. It has private rooms and dorms, all with shared bath. The owners also operate a great hostel in a quiet neighborhood in the suburb of East Coast. ◎ Map K4 • Block 5 Banda St. • 6323-3221 • www.fernloft.com • $

10 Prince of Wales
POWs, as it is known locally, is a popular hip bar and beer garden that hosts local bands. It also has adequate dorms and private rooms. Recommended for those who don't mind trading sleep for fun. ◎ Map F4 • 101 Dunlop St. • 6299-0130 • www.pow.com.sg • $

Recommend your favorite hotel on **traveldk.com**

General Index

Acknowledgments

The Authors

Susy Atkinson is a writer and freelance journalist. She has traveled widely in Asia and has contributed to several travel guides. Susy currently lives in Singapore.

Jennifer Eveland has spent 13 years in Asia, over 10 of them in Singapore. She has been writing professionally for over a decade, contributing to a range of publications on topics as varied as travel, fashion, finance, and politics.

Publisher
Douglas Amrine

List Manager
Christine Stroyan

Managing Art Editors
Mabel Chan, Sunita Gahir

Senior Editor
Sadie Smith

Project Editors
Justine Montgomery, Ros Walford

Project Designer
Nicola Erdpresser

Senior Cartographic Editor
Casper Morris

Senior Cartographer
Suresh Kumar

Cartographers
Stuart James, Schchida Nand Pradhan

Picture Researcher
Ellen Root

Picture Research Assistant
Rhiannon Furbear

DTP Operator
Natasha Lu

Production Controller
Sarah Hewitt

Photographer
Tony Souter

Additional Photography
Rough Guides/ Simon Bracken

Fact Checker
Jenny Tan

Americanization
Helen Townsend

Indexer
Helen Peters

Picture Credits
tl-top left; tc-top center; tr-top right; cla-center left above; cl-center left; c-center; cr-center right; cb-center below; bl-bottom left; bc-bottom center; br-bottom right.

Works of art have been reproduced with the kind permission of the following copyright holders: *Joy* Ruth Bloch 19tc.

The Publisher would like to thank the following individuals, companies and picture libraries for their kind permissions to reproduce their photographs: